D0866943

Praise for
Recovering from Religious Abuse

"Those who proclaim to come 'In the name of God' . . . should offer a message of truth in love. But not every leader does. Some hurt rather than heal. For those who have been pained by religious abuse—and it does happen—*Recovering from Religious Abuse* offers stirring thoughts, hope, and inspiration toward real 'freedom in Christ.'"

—Dr. Tim Clinton
President, American Association of Christian Counselors

"There is good news for those who turn away from God because of their experience of hurt and pain at the hands of Christian leaders and others in the body of Christ. The God of the universe, who loves and cares for us, should not be confused with those who have misrepresented Him. This practical and insightful book, *Recovering from Religious Abuse*, has been written to help you heal from the wounds you have received. Out of the caldron of personal experience, Jack Watts shares the insights of his journey in an easy-to-follow, yet powerful format. Follow the 91-day plan—one day at a time—and your life will be transformed in amazing ways. I highly recommend this book to those who have been wounded, as well as to the counselors who assist them."

—Joseph A. Kloba, Ed.D.
Provost & Chief Academic Officer
Professor of Counseling Psychology
Palm Beach Atlantic University

"The healing journey for those wounded by trusted spiritual leaders can be daunting. Clearly Jack has walked this road and blazed a trail for those who will follow."

—June Hunt
Founder, CEO & CSO
Hope for the Heart

"I began my journey of recovery from drug and alcohol addiction in February of 1971. I began my recovery from religious abuse in 1978. I wish

I would have had this book then. I have spent many years helping people find recovery from their hurts, habits, and hang-ups. During these years I have always looked for material that addresses the issues from both a clinical and a biblical perspective. Jack Watts has done that with this book. He also negotiates the fine line between showing compassion to the victimized (honor the struggle) and encouraging them to develop a victim mentality. If you have experienced this type of abuse, you are in danger of confusing God with the abuser. This recovery program will allow you to discover who God truly is in the person of Jesus Christ, without the baggage of the abuse. I heartily recommend this to fellow strugglers."

—Dr. Daryl Pitts, D. Min.
Pastor, Thomas Road Baptist Church
Adjunct Professor, Liberty University

"I've often heard it said that Christianity is the only army that shoots its wounded. For those of you who feel like you've been 'shot,' let me recommend *Recovering from Religious Abuse*. This practical, insightful book has been written to help you heal from the wounds you've received. It's a book that can help you regain your sense of purpose and be everything God created you to be."

—Matt Barnhill
Former Vice President, Rapha Treatment Centers
Care Ministries Pastor, Riverpoint Church

"Do you remember how joyful and hopeful you were when you first believed? That seems like a long time ago, doesn't it? This is especially true for those who have been wounded within Christendom—wounded by people they once trusted. That's why *Recovering from Religious Abuse* is such an important book. By working the 11 steps, disillusioned Christians can regain their sense of joy and purpose. It's a book every Christian should have in his or her bookcase."

—Orlando P. Peccora, MD

"Religious abuse is far more prevalent than most of us could ever imagine. Month after month during our Healing for the Nations Intensive Retreats, we see a number of people who struggle with the issue. Jack does a great job of presenting a recovery program that enables people to experience Jesus—seeing God for who He really is—not through the distorted lens abuse so often creates. This material is honest and real and encourages that kind of relationship with God. It is refreshing to see his understanding of clinical issues combined with discipleship and pastoral care. This material isn't focused on a victim mentality but, rather, victory in Christ. It offers more than just recovery; it offers growth, healing, and new life!"

—Rujon W. Morrison
Cofounder, Healing for the Nations

"Where do you turn when you've been wounded by a Christian leader? For those who have been abused—either verbally, emotionally, socially, financially, or sexually—you can turn to *Recovering from Religious Abuse,* which has been written specifically with you in mind. Jack's tough, no-nonsense approach is precisely what you may need to put your painful past behind you and move forward successfully with your life."

—Jim Baird
Director, B&H Academic

RECOVERING
FROM
RELIGIOUS ABUSE

11 Steps to Spiritual Freedom

JACK WATTS

 HOWARD BOOKS
A DIVISION OF SIMON & SCHUSTER, INC.

NEW YORK   NASHVILLE   LONDON   TORONTO   SYDNEY

Published by Howard Books, a division of Simon & Schuster, Inc.
1230 Avenue of the Americas, New York, NY 10020

First Howard Books hardcover edition February 2011

HOWARD and colophon are trademarks of Simon & Schuster, Inc.

For information about special discounts for bulk purchases,
please contact Simon & Schuster Special Sales at 1-866-506-1949 or
business@simonandschuster.com.

The Simon & Schuster Speakers Bureau can bring authors to your live event.
For more information or to book an event, contact the Simon & Schuster Speakers Bureau
at 1-866-248-3049 or visit our website at www.simonspeakers.com.

Designed by Kyoko Watanabe

Manufactured in the United States of America

10 9 8 7 6 5 4 3 2 1

Library of Congress Cataloging-in-Publication Data
Watts, Jack
    Recovering from religious abuse: 11 steps to spiritual freedom / Jack Watts.
        p. cm.
1. Psychological abuse victims—Religious life. 2. Sexual abuse victims—Religious life.
3. Psychological abuse—Religious aspects—Christianity. 4. Sex crimes—Religious aspects—
Christianity. 5. Recovery movement—Religious aspects—Christianity. 6. Spiritual life—
Christianity. I. Title.
    BV4596.P87W38 2011
    200.1'9—dc22
            2010024199

ISBN 978-1-4391-9268-9
ISBN 978-1-4391-9659-5 (ebook)

I have heard it said Christianity is the only army that shoots its wounded.
Like most aphorisms, this insight is right on target.
Recovering from Religious Abuse is dedicated to the millions of
Christian casualties, wounded by fellow believers.

CONTENTS

Contents

Contents

Contents

FOREWORD

In the twenty-first century, the church's focus is on experiencing and connecting more than on anything else. This focus creates significant problems.

While at church, a person's experiences provide pleasant memories but little true knowledge of God. Through connecting with other church people, a person is exposed to those who profess Christianity, but this type of association doesn't necessarily reveal much about God's true nature. Thus, attending church becomes a pleasant practice for many but has little substantive value.

Because of this shallow foundation, the church often acts like a dysfunctional family—with church leaders abusing those they profess to help. Leaders usually interpret what they do through "religious speak," which, in their own minds, exonerates them from any negative wrongdoing. This attitudes drives many away from church and away from God.

None of us lives well without God's being an integral part of our lives, which is especially true when we make the mistake of confusing other Christians with God—when we idolize those who profess to speak for Him. This kind of religious confusion occurs when people look to religious leaders for truth rather than to God.

This much-needed book is practical and, at the same time, goes straight to the place in a person's life where the heartache began. *Recovering from Religious Abuse* can be a tremendous help to those who still ache from abuse but yearn for a real, substantive relationship with God.

If we are to have the relationship with God that we yearn for, we must correct the problem abuse creates at the source. Sometimes we can go through long periods without realizing how much we need to hear from God. We can either go to Him to lead us through our difficult days, or we can go to others for help. We can utilize our own intellect, leaving God out of the process completely, or we can turn to Him. Unfortunately, due to religious abuse, many refuse to trust God, making their problems even worse.

For example, if I asked you if you have thoughts you don't want to think but which you thought anyway, you would probably say, "Yes, I have had those thoughts." If this condition is true of you—and it probably is— you have given your mind authority to think certain negative thoughts. Only God can destroy those thoughts. If you do not trust Him, you have no chance to control what you think.

If you'll recall, Satan's goal with Adam and Eve was to separate them from God by telling Eve that God was unfair. Many Christians find them- selves unwittingly aiding Satan's same goal today by exalting an image of God that is much more consistent with Satan than with God. Many of these Christians are leaders in the church.

Satan knows you are an easy target when you separate yourself from de- pendence on your heavenly Father. I have seen this scenario many times in the lives of those who have gone through satanic ritual abuse. The messages repeated over and over again by those tormenting these individuals—even when they were small children—were these:

- God does not really care for you.
- You have been ruined and will never be acceptable to God.
- God enjoys seeing you suffer.
- You cannot count on God.

Isn't it interesting that the results of religious abuse are the same as the goals of satanic ritual abuse?

When a person experiences religious abuse, one of the common results is stress. When stress takes over, sleep becomes a problem. Anger or sad- ness also becomes exaggerated. Depression slows thinking and responsive- ness to a crawl. It is no wonder that Jesus asked us to cast our cares upon Him—even the difficulties created by religious abuse.

Religious abuse is always legalistic and involves condemnation. Despite the clear teaching of Scripture—that there is to be "no condemnation" to those in Christ Jesus (see Romans 8:1)—the practitioners of religious abuse use condemnation as one of their primary tools. While accepting condemnation, the abused person doesn't believe he or she is worthy of God's love, care, and protection.

Practitioners of religious abuse can be, on the one hand, very reli- gious—pridefully so—while on the other hand rejecting the true mes- sage of salvation. They want to have the role of the Holy Spirit but bring a message that is anti-Christian. Instead of focusing on Christ and His forgiveness for your lifetime of sins, they want you to focus on them and what they tell you is acceptable or not.

They replace Christ with themselves. If you follow them, you will find yourself far removed from any experience of God's love and care for you.

If this is what has happened to you or to someone you care about, *Recovering from Religious Abuse* can help you get back on track. It can help you restore meaning and purpose to your life. It can point you back to God.

There is a story about a man who lived under a bridge for many years. His existence was painfully limited. One day he died, and those taking care of his funeral discovered his parents had left him a large inheritance, which had been available to him for many years. This question was asked at that point: "Was he a rich man or a poor man?" The answer was: "He was a rich man who had lived like a poor man most of his life."

The goal of religious abuse is to keep you living poorly—even though you should live richly because of your Father in heaven. *Recovering from Religious Abuse* will help you see how you've been led astray. More important, it will help you correct your course. It will help you be the person God created you to be. I recommend it wholeheartedly.

Robert S. McGee
Author, The Search for Significance

PREFACE

Writing *Recovering from Religious Abuse* required a little more than a year, but developing the 11 steps has necessitated a lifetime. Based on my own agonizing personal experience and that of others, each step has been carefully constructed to maximize the healing process for those who choose to do the work.

America is full of people who have experienced abuse of one kind or another. Because religious abuse also calls into question a person's relationship with God, it is particularly devastating. It's also the least discussed. That's why I've written *Recovering from Religious Abuse*. I want to help those who have been wounded by the church—by those who have chosen to use their positions of authority to use, abuse, and discard their fellow believers.

Most discarded Christians lead half-lives, consumed with pain, anger, shame, and bitterness. They question whether the best years of their lives have already passed, hoping they haven't but suspecting they have. They are prone to depression and to acting-out behaviors, including overeating, overspending, alcoholism, promiscuity, and many others.

The message I've tried to convey in *Recovering from Religious Abuse* is that the negative assessment given by an abuser, which becomes accepted and internalized as true, is a lie. God still loves abused people as much as ever—perhaps more. They can once again experience love, joy, kindness, and serenity—not just occasionally but routinely. The way is easy, but the work is challenging. Just like anything of value in life, the abused person has to work for it.

If this has been your experience and you want to regain the joy of your salvation, you can. *Recovering from Religious Abuse* can help you achieve your goal. In a very short time—91 days—you can become stronger than you ever thought possible, devoid of the chains that have imprisoned you since your abusive experience. I'm not guessing about this. I know it's true.

My hope is that you will work the steps and become everything God ever intended you to be. You can do it. God is on your side, and with Him as your ally, what's to stop you?

BEFORE YOU GET STARTED

Have I Been Religiously Abused?

What Is Religious Abuse?

Religious abuse is the mistreatment of a person by someone in a position of spiritual authority, resulting in the diminishing of that person's sense of well-being and growth—both spiritually and emotionally.

This spiritual authority is used to manipulate others for personal gain or to achieve a personal agenda, thereby harming that person's walk with God.

It can also be defined as any misuse of Scripture that harms a person's relationship with God—like the damage resulting from cult involvement.

A Self-Assessment Exercise

Have you experienced religious abuse? If so, how significant has it been? The following exercise will help you determine for yourself.

After reading each statement, simply circle the appropriate number on the ten-point scale. Try not to spend too much time on any one statement. Choose the first response that comes to your mind. Your gut reaction is usually the best.

Even if your abuse has been significant, there's hope for you. You can overcome the wounding you've experienced and become everything you're capable of being.

1. I have stopped going to church because someone in the ministry wounded me.

   10   9   8   7   6   5   4   3   2   1   0

   Strongly Agree / Agree / Neither Agree nor Disagree / Disagree / Strongly Disagree

2. Although mistreated by someone in the ministry, I still go to church, but I simply go through the motions.

   10   9   8   7   6   5   4   3   2   1   0

   Strongly Agree / Agree / Neither Agree nor Disagree / Disagree / Strongly Disagree

3. I believe God is displeased with me for leaving my church.

   10   9   8   7   6   5   4   3   2   1   0

   Strongly Agree / Agree / Neither Agree nor Disagree / Disagree / Strongly Disagree

4. I believe most Christians are hypocrites.

   10   9   8   7   6   5   4   3   2   1   0

   Strongly Agree / Agree / Neither Agree nor Disagree / Disagree / Strongly Disagree

5. Yes, a church leader has abused me.

   10   9   8   7   6   5   4   3   2   1   0

   Strongly Agree / Agree / Neither Agree nor Disagree / Disagree / Strongly Disagree

6. I feel unworthy to pray.

   10   9   8   7   6   5   4   3   2   1   0

   Strongly Agree / Agree / Neither Agree nor Disagree / Disagree / Strongly Disagree

7. I have been verbally abused by someone in the ministry.

   10   9   8   7   6   5   4   3   2   1   0

   Strongly Agree / Agree / Neither Agree nor Disagree / Disagree / Strongly Disagree

8. I have been sexually abused by someone in the ministry.

   10   9   8   7   6   5   4   3   2   1   0

   Strongly Agree / Agree / Neither Agree nor Disagree / Disagree / Strongly Disagree

9. I have been financially abused by someone in the ministry.

   10   9   8   7   6   5   4   3   2   1   0

   Strongly Agree / Agree / Neither Agree nor Disagree / Disagree / Strongly Disagree

10. I have been emotionally abused by a religious experience.

   10   9   8   7   6   5   4   3   2   1   0

   Strongly Agree / Agree / Neither Agree nor Disagree / Disagree / Strongly Disagree

11. I feel a sense of shame around religious people.

   10   9   8   7   6   5   4   3   2   1   0

   Strongly Agree / Agree / Neither Agree nor Disagree / Disagree / Strongly Disagree

12. I feel used by religious people.

   10   9   8   7   6   5   4   3   2   1   0

   Strongly Agree / Agree / Neither Agree nor Disagree / Disagree / Strongly Disagree

13. I believe religious people condemn me.

   10   9   8   7   6   5   4   3   2   1   0

   Strongly Agree / Agree / Neither Agree nor Disagree / Disagree / Strongly Disagree

14. I am angry with God.

   10   9   8   7   6   5   4   3   2   1   0

   Strongly Agree / Agree / Neither Agree nor Disagree / Disagree / Strongly Disagree

15. I feel unworthy to reach out to God.

   10   9   8   7   6   5   4   3   2   1   0

   Strongly Agree / Agree / Neither Agree nor Disagree / Disagree / Strongly Disagree

16. There is more to life than I'm experiencing.

    10   9   8   7   6   5   4   3   2   1   0

    Strongly Agree / Agree / Neither Agree nor Disagree / Disagree / Strongly Disagree

17. I would like to feel closer to God, but I don't believe it's possible.

    10   9   8   7   6   5   4   3   2   1   0

    Strongly Agree / Agree / Neither Agree nor Disagree / Disagree / Strongly Disagree

18. Life has no meaning.

    10   9   8   7   6   5   4   3   2   1   0

    Strongly Agree / Agree / Neither Agree nor Disagree / Disagree / Strongly Disagree

19. Sometimes I wonder if I have a drinking problem.

    10   9   8   7   6   5   4   3   2   1   0

    Strongly Agree / Agree / Neither Agree nor Disagree / Disagree / Strongly Disagree

20. Sometimes I wonder if I abuse prescription drugs.

    10   9   8   7   6   5   4   3   2   1   0

    Strongly Agree / Agree / Neither Agree nor Disagree / Disagree / Strongly Disagree

21. Sometimes I wonder if I have a problem with pornography.

    10   9   8   7   6   5   4   3   2   1   0

    Strongly Agree / Agree / Neither Agree nor Disagree / Disagree / Strongly Disagree

22. Sometimes I don't believe God loves me.

    10   9   8   7   6   5   4   3   2   1   0

    Strongly Agree / Agree / Neither Agree nor Disagree / Disagree / Strongly Disagree

Now that you've finished, add your total score.

- If you circled 7 or higher on any statement, *Recovering from Religious Abuse* can help you.
- If your total score is between 101 and 129, this book will help you.
- If you score 130 or above, you definitely need *Recovering from Religious Abuse*.
- If you score above 150, your need for *Recovering from Religious Abuse* is significant.

Four Personal Accounts of Religious Abuse

Religious abuse occurs frequently and can happen to anyone—regardless of gender, religious affiliation, or time of life. Most abuse is inadvertent—not intended to inflict permanent damage to a person. This is not the type of religious abuse we deal with in *Recovering from Religious Abuse*. Throughout this book, our focus is squarely upon those who use their positions of authority to abuse others, which makes it particularly devastating to the recipient. These leaders believe they have the authority and the right to do so. They believe they are entitled to treat others the way they do.

The consequences of their abusiveness are frequently catastrophic—nearly as devastating as when a parent tells a child that he or she is unloved and unwanted. Sadly, even little children can experience religious abuse at a time when they are the most vulnerable and impressionable. The negative imprint upon a child can last a lifetime, diminishing the recipient's self-worth. If unchecked, it can lessen a person's lifelong accomplishments.

Religious abuse is devastating because it nearly always brings the recipient's relationship with God into question. Either directly or indirectly, the abuser states or implies that the person's connection to God is flawed, making the abusee feel alienated—a person with diminished value, a person unworthy of God's love and care. Being estranged from God is like being estranged from a loving parent: no good comes from it.

To give you a better understanding—a better feel—for what religious abuse really is, four examples will be given: one from a small boy, one from an altar boy, one from a young man just beginning to make his way in the world, and one from a man going through a proverbial midlife crisis. Each is an example of a religious authority figure's using his position of power to abuse someone in his charge.

My own personal experiences with religious abuse are woven throughout all these stories, except for the one about the sexually abused altar boy. All are written in the first-person voice, showing the deeply personal nature of these abuses. After reading these accounts, perhaps you'll have a clearer picture of what religious abuse really is.

EXAMPLE ONE

Newton, Massachusetts: I grew up in the suburbs of Boston, the second of four children in an Irish-Catholic family. Being a good Catholic, I went to Mass every Sunday and each holy day of obligation, which meant I was in church at least sixty times a year. Some of my earliest memories are of being in church. Part of my education was in a Catholic school, which was challenging academically and good for me. Dealing with the nuns and priests, who were positioned as intermediaries between God and me, however, was difficult and not at all beneficial.

How they dealt with me has had an impact upon how I perceive God, which has influenced my entire life. I'm not alone; there are millions of Catholic kids like me who have their own stories to tell—many of which are much worse than mine.

One incident in particular had a profound impact on me. It was the day of my First Holy Communion when I was just seven years old. For months, all the girls and boys from my Communion class practiced going to the altar rail, kneeling down, holding our heads back, opening our mouths, and sticking out our tongues. When we did, the priest would put the Communion wafer on our tongues, say something that I couldn't understand, and move on to the next kid.

It sounds simple enough, but its execution on that fateful day was anything but simple. We were told—harshly, repeatedly, and in no uncertain terms—that we were to close our mouths immediately when the host was placed on our tongues.

The priest said, "You don't want to drop Jesus on the floor, do you?" He went on to tell us this was a sacrilege—a mortal sin—that would send us to hell. This, of course, terrified me as a seven-year-old. I can still feel the cold chill of fear from his words more than half a century later. His harsh admonition wasn't accurate Catholic teaching, but I didn't know it.

Although I was little, I remember trying to look at the wafer as the priest held it up. I wanted to see Jesus' face in it, but I never could. It didn't look like Him, and it didn't look like any part of a human being I had ever seen before either. Nevertheless, it was His body, and I was scared to death of dropping Jesus on the floor.

When the eventful day arrived, each girl was dressed in white, and all the boys, including me, wore white suits, white clip-on ties, and white gloves. Everything we wore that day was white, signifying purity—girls and boys. There were at least one hundred kids making their First Holy Communion that day, which seemed to excite the parents much more than it did any of us.

We sat up front away from our families—the boys on the right side of the aisle, the girls on the left. Sitting beside me was Jerry Callahan, who was a little goofy on his best day and slightly retarded on his worst. Because he was on my right, sitting right next to me, he was in line to receive Communion immediately before me.

On schedule, we were ushered to the rail by a nun. Each of us knelt precisely as we were instructed. When the priest came to Jerry, he didn't open his mouth as wide as he was supposed to. This irritated the priest, who spoke very sternly to him. Scared, Jerry started to whimper. Exasperated, the priest put the host on Jerry's partially protruding tongue, hoping all would go well.

Then the unthinkable happened: Jerry let the wafer drop from his mouth. Jesus landed on the floor right before my eyes. Aghast, the priest hurriedly grabbed the wafer, scraped up all the crumbs beside it, and put it in his own mouth, which really surprised me. After that, he rose quickly, gave Jerry a look of pure hate, and slapped him right across the face. It was a hard slap, and Jerry screamed from shock and pain.

As this drama was unfolding, Jerry's mother rushed forward to retrieve her child, who was now hysterical—screaming at the top of his lungs. As she arrived, she looked up at the priest and said, "I'm so sorry, Father." With that, she clutched her son, put a protective arm around his shoulder, and led him out of the church. I can still remember his receding sobs—as every adult looked at Jerry with contemptuous smirks.

The priest then turned his focus on me with defiant eyes, daring me to make a mistake. I was close to wetting my pants with fear, but I didn't. I did exactly as I was supposed to do. Because I was so afraid, however, my mouth was bone dry, and Jesus stuck to the roof of my mouth and wouldn't dissolve. It might as well have been peanut butter. Kids weren't allowed to talk with Jesus in their mouths, and we couldn't chew Him either. It was a sin. It took at least thirty minutes for Jesus to dissolve, and the Mass was long over before I could open my mouth and say a word.

The next year, Jerry died of a brain aneurysm. Because he was so traumatized by the priest's actions that day, he never was allowed to make his First Holy Communion. This meant he couldn't go to heaven, which saddened me. It's also why I have such a vivid memory of the incident so long after it occurred.

This episode solidified my fear of God or, more accurately, my terror of Him. I saw God as cold, hateful, impersonal, petty, and mean-spirited. He was punitive—just like the priest who gave me Communion that day. This twisted my perspective about God for years.

Everybody believed the priest had a right to do this, and nobody protested—not even Jerry's mother. Catholics were terrified of their priests—men who wielded unquestioned authority over the people in their parish. I can still feel the terror, which went deeper into my soul than the sacrament.

This incident was not isolated. It was routine in Roman Catholicism before Vatican II. If you think I'm wrong, just ask any Catholic who was raised during this era. Nearly every one of us has a story to tell about an abusive priest or nun. There are millions of stories to tell.

As I grew older and saw the world through adult eyes, I left the church. My memories of it are not pleasant. The mind-set of the Catholic clergy—at least the ones I knew—was that it was their right to slap kids around, and they did it routinely. Their power over the people was so strong and unassailable that moms and dads never protested how their children were being treated. This resulted in abuse that affected millions of kids like me—abuse that still impacts our lives. Just writing about it still angers me. I wonder if I'll ever get over it.

EXAMPLE TWO

Malden, Massachusetts: I can't remember a time when I wasn't expected to be an altar boy. My older brother—ten years my senior—had been one, and my mother talked about the day I would become one for as long as I can remember. It was expected of me, and my parents thought it was as important as getting good grades in school. I remember how badly I wanted to please my parents, and my only apprehension was whether or not I could learn the Latin responses well enough to "make the team."

When I was ten, I started learning the Mass, which was unintelligible and never made sense to me. I did everything I was expected to do, progressing satisfactorily. By the time I was eleven, I had become a first-rate altar boy and served with the parish priests every Sunday and each holy day of obligation, which were quite a few.

In the spring, just before my twelfth birthday, a new priest came to our parish, and he was much more friendly than the others, especially to me. I was his favorite altar boy, by far. I liked him a lot, even though he was heavy and always smelled like a chimney because of all the cigarettes he smoked. He always took time to talk to me, and when I was serving with him, I really liked being an altar boy—his altar boy.

After the last Mass one day, however, after Father had been there about six months, he asked me to stay behind for a while because he wanted to talk to me. Naturally, I did as he asked. We were in the back room, which was reserved for the priests and altar boys to prepare for Mass. While I was standing at the window looking out, Father came up behind me, reached around me with his right hand, holding me tight but not hurting me. Then he reached into my pants with his left hand and touched me. I was really surprised. I never dreamed he would do something like that. When he did, I froze. I didn't know what to do, and I was scared to death. Because he was a priest, I didn't challenge him, which I suppose I should have done, but I had just turned twelve. A kid like me could never challenge a priest. When I went home, I didn't say a word to my mother, either. I just couldn't. I was too embarrassed.

When I went back to serve the next week, he asked for me to stay after Mass again, which I obediently did. Once again, he touched me, which I knew he would. This time, however, he did more than that—much more than that. This little scenario went on for quite a while, but I never said a word. When we were alone after Mass and I knew it was time, I would just walk over toward the window with my back turned and wait for him to come to me, which he always did.

Honestly, this is the part I hate to admit. After a while, I didn't mind it any more. I liked it, and he knew I did, which meant our secret would always remain safe. This went on for more than a year. Then, one day, he stopped. I never served Mass with him again, and I was never alone with him again either. This really confused me, and I was ashamed of myself for missing "our time together" so much. Another boy from my neighborhood, who was a couple of years younger than I, took my place.

All that happened decades ago, but it still bothers me. It didn't make me homosexual. It did just the opposite. It made me hate gays, and it also made me hate God for allowing a pedophile priest to molest me. I know God's real, but I haven't been to Mass for decades. That experience, which remained bottled up inside me for years, has caused me problems my whole life—just ask my two ex-wives or my three sons, none of whom I ever allowed to be altar boys. No way!

EXAMPLE THREE

Atlanta, Georgia: I was really wild in college. While at the University of Georgia in Athens, I drank a lot, always had girls hanging around, and gambled routinely at my fraternity house. For a while it was fun, but it also made me feel like I was wasting my life. Because of this, I went to a Campus Crusade for Christ meeting, received Christ as my savior, and began to change my life for the better. I abandoned my wild side, which made me feel much better about myself.

After moving to Atlanta, I spent a great deal of time at church—more than I had ever spent in my entire life. I went to a very conservative church where they made me a Sunday-school teacher for the ninth grade. The kids loved me. I was young, handsome, energetic, interesting, and fun—exactly what these kids wanted to be like when they went to college.

One day during class, a girl asked me, "Should I square-dance as a part of the school curriculum or make a stand for Christ because dancing is sinful?"

Totally surprised by the question, I replied, "Why would you want to look ridiculous in front of everybody in school over square dancing? If I were you, I would just go ahead and do it. If you're going to make a stand, make it about something important—not something trivial."

Satisfied with my answer, I went on with the lesson. That night I received a call from the church pastor. He said, "I want to ask you some questions about your position on some critical issues for teens." Sensing the underlying malice in his silky tone, I listened intently as he asked me my position on movies, dancing, cards, and numerous other things. Finally, he said, "What's your position on mixed bathing?"

11

Without hesitation, I responded, "I'm against it. I think it's okay for boys and girls to swim together, but I'm dead set against them taking a bath together!" Complete silence ensued. My attempt to interject a little humor into a tense situation actually made things worse.

"I think we need to have lunch tomorrow," he said. "Can you meet me at twelve thirty?" It wasn't a request.

At 12:30 I met the pastor, a man in his midthirties with jet-black hair, pale white skin, and penetrating beady eyes. As we sat down, I was very nervous and started to light a Marlboro. In his most ingratiating voice, the pastor said, "It's alright if you smoke. I'll love you just as much if you light that cigarette as I will if you don't." When he finished saying this, he smiled in a genuine and disarming way.

"I know. Thanks," I said and lit the cigarette. Enraged, he seethed with anger as I sat there speechless. He lit into me for smoking in the first place and went on with a tirade that would draw approbation from any prosecutor in the land. I sensed pure hate in this man toward me as he verbally undressed me from head to toe. He said no one who was genuinely a Christian smoked, which meant I wasn't really a Christian in the first place. This really surprised me. Because he knew the Bible much better than I, I assumed he was correct. When he was finished, I was devastated. I held my ground outwardly, but inwardly I cringed—liked a whipped dog.

Incredulously, I asked, "Then why did you say it was alright to smoke?"

His reply was a contemptuous smirk—nothing more.

In truth, he couldn't answer. It would have been too revealing. At the end of the meal, he prayed and left with the self-satisfied confidence that he had set another sinner straight.

After he left, I was shaken to the core. I had been a born-again Christian for less than six months, but I knew I never wanted to be like this self-righteous, mean-spirited pastor. It bothered me so much that since then I have never been able to tolerate such misanthropy—especially from those who parade their Christianity as their prime asset. I went to that church less frequently and finally stopped going altogether. I became cautious and guarded around church people rather than open and transparent. I remember thinking that Christians shouldn't talk about loving people if they don't practice what they preach.

When I went to his church, I was young and impressionable. I eventually stopped smoking, but the effects of my confrontation have been far more detrimental than anything the cigarettes could have caused. As the pastor, he had every right to question what I taught the kids, but he had no right to crush my spirit. My enthusiasm for Christianity waned, and I have remained guarded and cautious ever since. Stung by his verbal abuse, I have never trusted pastors again—not completely. I'm sure he intended to help, but he didn't. Instead he used his authority to assault my self-worth—a strategy that worked to my detriment for years.

EXAMPLE FOUR

Santa Clara, California: Life in my church was like a soap opera—with all the excitement and intrigue you would expect from any daytime TV show. Some of my friends and I actually joked about it, saying, "This is just another day in *As the Stomach Turns*."

The reason there was so much drama is simple: the church had turned into a cult by replacing several core elements of Christianity with authoritarian rule by a group of "self-appointed" elders. The man who started the church insisted upon this change, and most of the people submitted to it, including me. It was more like a cult of personality than a church, because the leaders, who were called "The Elders," took on the founder's personality traits—especially the angry, confrontational, and profane ones.

Our church didn't start out like this, but it changed when the founder changed—when his personality changed. He was no longer the energetic, friendly, charismatic man I had met years earlier. In a short period of time, he transformed into a petty, vindictive, cruel tyrant. His tongue was acerbic and extremely critical. He took particular delight in criticizing women, especially his wife, who became a shell of what she had once been. As the mother of his many children, she would never divorce him. Instead, she left him mentally and emotionally, retreating into a world of trivial dithering. It was her only escape. The confident, capable woman I once knew no longer existed.

The founder's unkindness also extended to me, hurting me very deeply. In the beginning I was highly valued, but that changed practically overnight. I never understood what caused this change in him—still don't—but the change was real, and I felt it acutely.

Instead of exhibiting love and joy, which typified us for years, our church became characterized by fear, anger, intimidation, condemnation, and verbal abuse. To counteract any criticism, The Elders "dealt with the sin in the camp." They did this by paying a visit, usually without warning, to an unsuspecting person who needed straightening out. They would sit the person down and shout at him or her, demanding change and compliance. They would start the meeting by saying something like this: "You know what you are? You're a worthless piece of s——; that's what you are. I wonder why the f—- we even bother with you." From there, it would only get worse. By the time they left, the person was an emotional cripple—ready to do whatever he or she was told.

You might question, *Why would anybody in his or her right mind put up with this?* There were two reasons: First, we lived in a bizarre situation. As a "house church" in a hippie community during the Vietnam War, things didn't seem as weird or as abusive as they actually were. Second, if you didn't submit to The Elders, your entire family was excommunicated—shunned and treated with contempt and humiliation. This meant, for example, that your kids couldn't play with their friends from the church anymore and many other similar, petty acts of social cruelty. For example, a person being "dealt with" by The Elders would be forbidden to attend a potluck, so that everybody could talk about the person and make jokes at his or her expense. They even made one man stand in the corner for an hour like he was a five-year-old. Most people complied. The social ostracizing of the others was truly painful to watch.

The founder and another man started calling themselves apostles and said that church tradition, particularly from Orthodox churches, was as authoritative as Scripture. I couldn't understand this; it seemed like such a radical departure from our past. Most of the leadership had been from Baptist or charismatic churches, and now they wanted to wear collars like priests. What was being taught was the polar opposite of what had been taught a decade earlier.

I was badly confused and didn't know what to do or how to handle what was happening. While in this confused state of mental turmoil, I flew back east for my sister's wedding, leaving my wife and children in Santa Clara. To save money, I stayed at my brother's house.

My friend's neighbor, who I'll call Melissa, took care of my friend's young sons so that we could have a pleasant evening and stay at the reception longer. It was nice to be with my family and lifelong friends. Because it was an escape from all the stress at home, I let my guard down and became extremely intoxicated. My judgment also was impaired.

For years, Melissa had had a crush on me. After my friend and his wife went to bed, Melissa made her move. Well, you can guess what happened. We had an encounter, at the end of which I freaked out. I dressed, left the house, and walked for hours. My life was in shambles, and I knew it. I called my wife and told her exactly what had happened—all of it. I was desperate for help. Her response, which I expected, was to call The Elders.

When I returned to Santa Clara the following day, The Elders were waiting for me—all of them. I wasn't allowed to go home until they "dealt with me." When I arrived, I had never felt so heartsick and remorseful in my life. I was willing to do anything to get back on track. The Elders could see this, but it didn't matter. They only had one method for handling every situation—abusive verbal intimidation. After two hours of enduring their malicious condemnation, I started having suicidal ideations for the first time in my life. Shattered and intimidated, I became very compliant.

Their verbal abuse was difficult to handle. Far worse, however, was their chiding and contemptuous ridicule, which never ended. By contrast, confession in Roman Catholicism is sacred, and nothing said is ever repeated. At our church, the exact opposite was true. Confession to The Elders was fuel for gossip, providing another level of disgrace and humiliation. They also kicked me off the softball team—to give me more time "to think about" what I had done.

There were four sets of elders, and each set had responsibility for at least fifteen families. The elders for our family were, by far, the most brutal at the church. One was a plumber, and the other was a gardner. Both had graduated high school but had no further education. I was expected to "submit" every important personal and family decision to them to see if it was God's will or not. To this day, I can still see them wagging a finger at me—with dirt under their fingernails—to tell me angrily, without question, what God's will was for my life.

For example, when I decided to get an MA and a PhD, they were my authority concerning educational matters. The plumber could barely read, but he was God's authority in my life about higher education. Nearly everybody accepted this nonsense. If you questioned it, your loyalty and submissiveness quickly became the issue, and you were "dealt with accordingly." In other words, they would scream at you, routinely using profanity to do so—while at the same time calling it God's will.

They actually practiced a de facto infallibility because they never would admit to being wrong about how they handled a situation. They would always say they made a lot of mistakes, but no mistake was ever specific.

This is how a cult works and how it exercises power over the young, the naive, and the unstable, which was nearly everybody in our church.

Over time and slowly, The Elders became the head of the household in each family, usurping authority that rightfully belonged to the husband. It's how they maintained an iron fist of control. They were like the pigs in *Animal Farm* who ended up dressing like men, calling themselves more equal than the other animals. I knew it was wrong and clearly undermined the sanctity of each family, but nearly all of my friends accepted it as gospel. I couldn't. To me, it was aberrant, and I found myself at the library every day, reading about cults and brainwashing.

I began writing about what life was really like in our church and submitted it to the leaders as a critique for much-needed reform. It took me a year to complete; I'm not sure the founder even read it. Presenting it to him and the others, however, was very important for me, because I wasn't going to be bullied by their cultic practices any longer, nor would I allow them to verbally abuse me ever again.

I finally broke free from the cult, but the years of abusiveness took a heavy toll on my wife and me. She had a difficult time recovering emotionally from our experience in the cult, which undermined our marriage.

I became an alcoholic and had a string of relationships. Like a self-fulfilling prophecy, I became the person The Elders said I would be. I stopped believing God loved me, and I was very angry with Him for many years. My self-worth was in the toilet, and it required a decade for me to figure out what happened. When I did, I did the work necessary to finally get back on track—to reestablish my relationship with God. To this day, however, it's hard to be a member of a church. I can't let my guard down completely—I just can't. The damage is too deep.

In each of these cases, religious abuse occurred. Obviously, the priest had no right to slap a seven-year-old child. In the second case, the priest's abuse was far greater than any of the other examples, causing pain and confusion, which has adversely impacted the abused person ever since. There is no greater abuse than to sexually violate another, especially a child. In the third example, the minister used his position of authority to assault the young man's character instead of dealing with the issue, which in that case was the church's belief that square dancing was sinful. In this instance, the abuse was probably unintentional. The abuse in the final case, however, was more serious. In fact, it was life altering and very destructive. Not many suffer abuse at this level, but those who do have significant scarring to their souls.

Tragically, religious abuse occurs every day, and millions have stories bottled up inside them. Perhaps you have one as well? Even if you consider your abuse to be minor, it is an issue that needs to be addressed. This is specifically what *Recovering from Religious Abuse* will help you accomplish.

Who Will Benefit from
Recovering from Religious Abuse?

If you're looking at *Recovering from Religious Abuse* for the first time, you may wonder whether reading this book will be worthwhile or not—something that could benefit you. Obviously, that is a good question. Your score on the self-assessment exercise will help you determine how substantial your abuse has been, but in your heart, you probably already know the answer. You can feel it. If your life has changed from what it once was, from what you thought it would be, *Recovering from Religious Abuse* can help you. If your negative experience has filled you with self-pity, if you experience little fulfillment, if you are grinding out your days in mediocrity—with little love, meaning, or joy—this book can help you regain what you've lost. If you've had any of these feelings and know deep inside that you're not living the quality of life you're meant to live, *Recovering from Religious Abuse* is definitely for you.

This recovery program has been created for disenfranchised Christians and those in recovery groups like Alcoholics Anonymous, ALANON, Overeaters Anonymous, and sex-and-love-addiction recovery groups. It's specifically for wounded, hurting people who want more from life; it's for those who want fulfillment.

Taking you through 11 concrete steps, this simple program can help you recover from any type of abuse—including spousal abuse—but it's primarily targeted for those who have experienced religious abuse. Religious abuse is a massive problem in our society, which religious leaders have historically refused to acknowledge—let alone address. It's rare for church leaders to give more than lip service to religious abuse. Most routinely dismiss it as a minor issue.

They're mistaken. It's a substantial problem, adversely affecting millions. If you're one of the walking wounded, you've felt the pain, experienced the shame, and tasted the betrayal. You understand the significance of the problem. Once you've experienced it, you never forget. The pain eventually diminishes, but the scars never heal—not completely. They can leave you unable to interact spontaneously, as you once did. If this has been your experience, there's hope for you. You can experience a quality of life you thought was lost forever. Take some time each day for three months—just 91 days. Reconnect with God in a rich, healing way—a way that will restore purpose and meaning to your life. You will smile at the future once again, knowing that God is leading you each step of the way.

This program is simple, but it's not easy. It's hard work, requiring soul-searching honesty. If you're diligent, however, you'll regain your vision and purpose. Although abusiveness may have robbed you of your joy, God wants to restore all that has been lost, enriching your life in the process. Remember, it wasn't God who abused you. The abuse came from misguided people who used God's name in vain. Jesus was abused by religious leaders—just like you have been. He knows how you feel. He knows how to care for you, and He has the power to restore you to wholeness.

Are you ready for a change? Are you tired of living in fear, apprehensive of the future? Are you weary of spinning your wheels—alienated from God, discouraged, and devoid of vision? Do you want the richness you once possessed reinstated to you? Would you like your self-worth and self-confidence restored as well?

If your answer to these questions is yes, isn't it time to come home and rekindle the relationship you've put on the back burner for so long? If your heart yearns to be everything God intended you to be, then *Recovering from Religious Abuse* is definitely for you.

Having felt each of the debilitating emotions you've experienced, I know the value of recovery—the value of these 11 steps. I've experienced feelings of rejection, disappointment, anger, and despair—even suicidal thoughts. Because I accepted the condemning statements made about me by my accusers, I spent years without purpose—living in shame, disconnected, and fearful. I internalized my accusers' ridicule—as if it were true, as if it came from God Himself, which it definitely did not. Believing a lie, I acted out the role of an unloved, unwanted Christian and paid a heavy price for it. Like a self-fulfilling prophecy, I became what my abusers accused me of being, behaving badly and wasting years in pursuit of fruitless goals.

Like you, my abusers sought my destruction, but God used the events to strengthen me, to allow my experience to have value for others—perhaps for someone like you. Decades later, I stand strong, resilient, purposeful, and at peace. So can you.

Having walked a hard road, which led nowhere, I want to impart the wisdom I've gained while living in the desert. Having learned from my experience and successfully rekindled my first love, I want to share some principles that work—a way to return joy, purpose, and fulfillment to your life; a way free from guilt, shame, and depression. If you have medicated your pain with alcohol, drugs, pornography, sex, food, or self-pity, the 11 steps can help you change your self-destructive lifestyle. It's what *Recovering from Religious Abuse* is all about.

How to Benefit Most from *Recovering from Religious Abuse*

For the next 91 days, you will find targeted entries—each specifically created to touch different areas of your life. Because they are sequential, the best results will be obtained by working them in order. The days are also progressive—designed to help you deal with the underlying issues that block your recovery.

The first week introduces the concept of recovery, which may be new for many of you. Because we are not dealing with an addiction like alcoholism, where there is a behavior that has to be abandoned, the effects of abuse can be more difficult to recognize.

After the introductory week, each week will focus on one step for the next eleven weeks, to be followed by a concluding week. Sunday's reading introduces the week's material to follow. Each subsequent day is highly structured. Start by reading the step. Read it audibly each day to become more familiar with what it says. For those in recovery, the 11 steps are not only action steps, they are similar to proven aphorisms—providing wisdom, discernment, and guidance. Learn to make them a part of your life. They will guide you during difficult times.

The *reading* follows. If something strikes you, stop, pause, and meditate. Be as reflective as you desire. It will deepen your understanding as you begin the recovery process. Be certain to read the scripture at the close of the reading section, which ties directly to the reading and the step you're working. It's the synergy between each component that allows one day to build upon the previous one, making the process truly rewarding.

When you *pray*, do so audibly, adding as many of your thoughts and words as you desire to the written prayer. Remember, prayer is communication with God, and He is the only One who has the power to change you. *Writing* is essential, and you should take time each day for it—like something you check off a to-do list.

Finally, thoughtfully *reflect* on the scriptures at the end of each step.

If you commit quality time to your recovery, you will be amazed at the progress you make. By spending ten to twenty minutes a day, which is a small investment for a significant reward, your life should transform. By doing the work honestly and consistently, your life will change for the better—no doubt about it. With this in mind, let's begin!

11 Steps to Spiritual Freedom

1. I acknowledge that my life is shipwrecked and not where I want it to be.

2. I commit to stop living my life in pursuit of self-defeating behavior.

3. I accept that the responsibility for getting back on track is mine and no one else's.

4. I choose to believe what God says about Himself: that He is good and can be trusted. I recognize that God is not the abuser; rather, people who misuse their authority are the abusers.

5. I recognize that the only way back to a productive life is exactly the way I came. Therefore, I commit to repairing my relationship with God and making amends with everyone I have wronged along the way.

6. I refuse to become like those who have abused me, and I abandon my desire to spread malice because of my pain and my anger.

7. I will make a detailed, written account of my abusive experiences as well as my subsequent behavior. I commit to being as thorough and honest as I'm able.

8. I will share my experience and my own wrongdoing with a trusted friend, confessing the exact state of my heart.

9. I humbly ask God to change anything He wishes, and I ask Him to heal my pain. Because God forgives us as we forgive others, I forgive my abusers.

10. I choose to believe God still has a purpose for my life—a purpose for good and not evil.

11. I make a commitment to nurture my relationship with God, asking Him to reveal His will to me and to give me the power to carry it out.

A New Life of
Spiritual Freedom Awaits You

Your life isn't over. Neither is your purpose for living. You can be stronger than you ever imagined and become a better person, by far, than you've ever been. God still has a plan for you—a plan full of hope and purpose, a plan for good things, not bad. It's waiting for you.

All that's missing is your willingness to reach out for it, doing the necessary work to recover. It's the key to unleashing God's power in your life. Unless you actively participate, however, nothing will happen.

If you are willing—even desirous, all things are possible. Hope, once again, will become a significant part of your life; and nothing—not your abuser, your circumstances, nor hell itself—can stand in your way. If God is with you—and He is—who can stand against you?

A NEW BEGINNING

Introduction

In the United States, there are recovery groups for alcoholics, drug addicts, sex addicts, overeaters, overspenders, and numerous other subgroups with unique recovery needs. All are needed, but there is another group that also requires help: those who have been abused by organized religion—primarily by religious leaders in positions of trust.

With these abused people in mind, *Recovering from Religious Abuse* has been developed. Helping people like you to recover is my purpose—my only purpose.

Each of the following 91 readings, which lead you through the "11 Steps to Spiritual Freedom," has been developed to help those who have suffered—or continue to suffer—from religious exploitation. There are millions of you—people who have been used, abused, and discarded—dismissed contemptuously by those you trusted completely, suffering shame and low self-esteem in the process.

Most of you are bitter and resentful. You may even be hostile. If you are, that's okay. We accept you right where you are—without reservation or condemnation. Having been wronged in the past, you may have discarded your belief in God, or perhaps you've put Him on the back burner.

It's easy to understand how this could happen, but it's also self-defeating behavior. God is a part of the solution, not a part of the problem. It's like saying, "I'll get even with You; I'll hurt me." Obviously, this isn't a good idea, but it's what millions have done.

If it's what you've been doing, you don't have to continue. You can make a change. There's a way out that works, and *Recovering from Religious Abuse* can help you find your way back to wholeness—back to emotional and spiritual wellness. That's why I've written this book. I want to help you recover. I want to help you become the best person you can possibly be, and I want to show you how to free yourself from bitterness, resentment, shame, and other debilitating emotions, all of which lead to an unfulfilled life.

If you're angry with God, that's not surprising. Most abused people are—whether they are willing to admit it or not. It's not unexpected; it's predictable. But remember, Christ also was abused by religious leaders— just like you have been. He was accused falsely; then He was slandered, beaten, and murdered. Obviously, He understands how you feel—precisely how you feel. When you think about it, He never had much use for self-righteous religious leaders either, did He?

Just because you've been wronged, however, doesn't mean it's acceptable to sit on the sidelines and wallow in self-pity, nurturing a self-indulgent belief that life has mistreated you. That's not taking good care of yourself. A life of resentment or smoldering, camouflaged bitterness is a wasted existence. I'm here to help you change that—if it's something you want. Your willingness to change is the key. No one else can have that desire for you. Not even God can do that. You have to make the effort to help yourself. You have to want it.

If you will make even the slightest attempt to open your heart—to be willing to change—recovery can begin. If you start moving toward God, you will find Him to be everything you ever dreamed Him to be. After all, it's God who heals broken hearts. He can heal yours. Will you make the effort?

Still Living in Denial?

Read: If you've made the decision to compartmentalize Christianity—to keep God at arm's length—you have essentially thrown out the baby with the bath water, neutralizing God's power in your life. When you discarded Christianity, or at least most of it, you probably were surprised that so few negative consequences followed—at least not at first. You walked away, and God just allowed you to leave. He didn't chase after you—even though it broke His heart to see you go.

God never chases after anyone and always honors an individual's decision to stay or wander away. Free will is not a doctrine; it's reality—your reality. When you chose to shelve Christianity, perhaps throwing stones as you abandoned it, God honored your right to do so. There's something noble about that. God respected your decision and treated you like an adult—even when your behavior may have been foolish and childish.

Leaving was not the end of the story, however. It was probably just the beginning. You may think you're done with God, but He's not done with you—not by a long shot. Because His Spirit lives in you, He has a huge stake in your future—in who you become. For a while, you probably enjoyed being finished with Christianity, but life has a way of coming full circle. Like the prodigal son, pursuing materialism and vice is not as rewarding as you thought it would be, is it?

Has God orchestrated your circumstances to make your life less than meaningful, or is it worse than that? Are you miserable or just bored? Are you tired of suffering the consequences of poor behavior—of being half dead while still being alive?

Do you own enough of your soul to admit the reality of your situation, or do you still live in a state of denial, telling yourself you're okay—you're fine the way you are? Are you finished running, or do you need to wander for a while longer?

When you come to the end of yourself—when you've bottomed out—there's no place to go but home, home to your heavenly Father. At the end of your anger and your rebelliousness, there is nothing but sorrow and pain—a life unfulfilled and wasted. You're not where you belong, and you know it.

Come home, not to meaningless religion or more abusiveness, but to a deep, fulfilling relationship with God Himself. He's waiting; it's time.

I am with you always, even to the end of the age. (MATTHEW 28:20)

Pray: Father, I'm tired of feeling empty. Please lead me back to You. I want to come home, but I'm not sure how to get there. It's time; help me come back to where I belong.

Write: Spend time today considering what it would mean for you to "come home." Take time to journal about this concept.

Reflect

When he came to his senses, he said, "How many of my father's hired men have more than enough bread, but I am dying here with hunger! I will get up and go to my father, and will say to him, 'Father, I have sinned against heaven, and in your sight; I am no longer worthy to be called your son; make me as one of your hired men.'" So he got up and came to his father. But while he was still a long way off, his father saw him and felt compassion for him, and ran and embraced him and kissed him. And the son said to him, "Father, I have sinned against heaven and in your sight; I am no longer worthy to be called your son." But the father said to his slaves, "Quickly bring out the best robe and put it on him, and put a ring on his hand and sandals on his feet; and bring the fattened calf, kill it, and let us eat and celebrate; for this son of mine was dead and has come to life again; he was lost and has been found." And they began to celebrate.

—LUKE 15:17–24

You've Had Dark Times

Read: Each of the readings in this book is authentic—without sugar coating. That's a promise. Because we've heard so many "war stories," the material is based on what's real—not what's imagined. Regardless of your particular situation, others have had similar experiences and have recovered to lead fruitful lives—lives of value.

God loves you just the way you are—despite your circumstances, despite your state of mind. He doesn't see you as others see you or as you see yourself. His insight into you is penetrating and accurate. He knows you've experienced dark times and have made self-defeating choices, but He loves you exactly the way you are—even though you may not love yourself. You can count on it. It's true, and it's not going to change.

Your life still has incredible value. If you choose to experience God's accepting, forgiving touch once again, you'll want to take your rightful place as a favored child—a child with promise. Having been derailed will no longer thwart your future, a future that can be full of hope and promise. Like Israel after the Holocaust, you will learn to say with confidence, "never again" to spiritual abuse.

That's my goal for you: to help you heal and become the mature man or woman God destined you to be—emotionally sound and resilient. Your entire outlook on life will change, as will your attitude. Steadfast confidence will replace despair and the defeated life you've been living for so long.

Aren't you tired of being cynical and pessimistic? It's so fatiguing. Besides, God doesn't need more cynics; He already has more than He can use.

Isn't it time to make some changes? Wouldn't it be nice to be filled with love, joy, peace, patience, and kindness once again? But this time, you could add wisdom to the list. Your life can be one of calm, strong sanity. This is not a "name it, claim it" approach to life. Recovery requires real work, real faith, real commitment, and time. If you work for it, however, you will be amazed by the progress you make, and so will others. That's the promise recovery brings—a new life, a better life.

*And because we are his children, God has sent the Spirit of his
Son into our hearts, prompting us to call out, "Abba, Father."*
(GALATIANS 4:6 NLT)

Pray: God, lead me as I pursue this path of recovery. Strengthen me as I
begin this journey.

Write: Prepare yourself for the days ahead. Start journaling about this
new beginning. Ask God for help—moment by moment—and surround
yourself with people who will be encouraging in this process. Talk to one
or two friends who will be supportive, and tell them you are beginning
Recovering from Religious Abuse.

Reflect

*I am convinced that neither death, nor life, nor angels, nor
principalities, nor things present, nor things to come, nor powers, nor
height, nor depth, nor any other created thing, will be able to separate
us from the love of God, which is in Christ Jesus our Lord.*

—ROMANS 8:38–39

Slip Sliding Away

Read: When you started moving away from God—whether consciously or unconsciously—you began to compromise who you were. At first, it may have been just a thing or two, followed by another and then another. Before long, much of who you were—what made you strong, purposeful, and resilient—no longer existed. You became a vestige of your former self, but you still maintained the illusion that you were okay. People who react to religious abuse do this all the time, denying how far they have drifted—especially to themselves.

You could still talk the talk, but if you're being honest, you'll admit you began gravitating to the darker side of life rather than toward the Light.

Does this sound familiar? Take a moment and think about it.

Have little pieces of your character been shaved off one at a time? Do you wonder if there's anything left? Does reading this cause you discomfort? Is it painful to introspect at such a tender, vulnerable level? Is it all you can do to continue? Do you want to walk away and think about something else?

If so, you are precisely where you need to be. It's the place where you begin to see the difference between who you pretend to be and who you really are. Others may tell you how wonderful you are, but you know it's not entirely true. Their approbation doesn't match how you feel inside, does it?

You're probably not even close to where you want to be—not on the inside anyway. Your success, as measured by the state of your self-approval, is far less than it should be.

If all of this is true, then you're in a place where God's healing touch should be very desirable. There's nothing like it. All you need to do is stop walking away from Him, turn around, and start walking back toward Him. When you do, He will be more than you ever imagined, strengthening you with peace, motivation, and direction.

If you are sick and tired of being sick and tired, call upon your heavenly Father. If you have reached a place where you are willing to bend your knee and cry out for help, God will hear you. Out of your despair, He will answer you—you can count on it. *There is life after abuse—a rewarding life, a fulfilling life.*

When you're ready, so is God.

Jesus was going through all the cities and villages, teaching in their synagogues and proclaiming the gospel of the kingdom, and healing every kind of disease and every kind of sickness. (MATTHEW 9:35)

Pray: Father, I admit I am not where I want to be or where I should be. Please do what it requires to get me back on the right track. Bring Your healing into my life, and make me whole.

Write: Carve out a few minutes to spend alone with God. Use this time to reflect on and journal about who He is, His love for you, and His desire to heal you.

Reflect

Do not be wise in your own eyes;
Fear the LORD and turn away from evil.
It will be healing to your body
And refreshment to your bones.

—PROVERBS 3:7–8

The Negative Power
of Self-Pity

Read: Denial is a state of mind that maintains, "Everything is just fine," when it obviously isn't. At the other end of the spectrum is another state of mind, which is equally debilitating. It's self-pity, which rivals denial in keeping a person emotionally shackled. Those in denial refuse to believe they need help; those who are gripped by self-pity believe they are helpless.

It's easy to see how someone abused can feel sorry for himself or herself. At one time or another, nearly every abused person has a problem with self-pity. It's a huge stumbling block to recovery.

When abuse occurs, especially by a religious leader, the abusee feels victimized, hurt, and angry. Over time, the intensity of the pain diminishes, leaving the individual with a lingering feeling of rejection—based on unfair and unwarranted treatment. Because of the unfairness, the person's attitude often deteriorates into self-pity, which is a particularly difficult perspective to reverse. It's a defeatist mind-set that is nurtured and fed by those who possess it. Sadly, those who are given to self-pity come to embrace it. In their pain, they nurture their heartache as they come to delight in adversity, believing it is their fate.

They fall into a negative rut and rarely look at life optimistically. They can recite every wrong perpetrated upon them, citing chapter and verse flawlessly. Their pain becomes their pleasure as they apply a pessimistic interpretation to every blessing that comes their way. When you're with someone who indulges in self-pity, that person often casts a negative emotional penumbra upon everyone present, draining energy from all of them. By nurturing self-pity, the person abandons reality and refuses to take responsibility for his or her life.

Recovery for these people is very difficult because they cherish their dysfunction, calling it normal and enlightened. Suffering is their lot in life—like Jesus. It's what God has called them to—just ask them. They adamantly believe this.

Like alcoholics, those committed to overcoming self-pity have to live life one day at a time, rejecting the tendency to embrace self-pity as their emotional opiate. It can be done, but it's extremely difficult. If you have a problem with self-pity, you'll have to work particularly hard.

*If we claim we have no sin, we are only fooling ourselves and not
living in the truth. But if we confess our sins to him, he is faithful
and just to forgive us our sins and to cleanse us from all wickedness.*
(1 JOHN 1:8–9 NLT)

Pray: God, show me my heart. If there is any self-pity there, please help me recognize it for what it is. Give me the courage to admit the truth to myself and to You.

Write: Frequently, self-pity and denial become a way of life. If this is the case, it can be difficult to see these traits in yourself. Ask God to show you where they exist, or ask a trusted friend if he or she sees these characteristics in you. Be open to the answer you receive, and resist the inclination to be defensive. Journal about any revelations God gives you.

Reflect
Search me, O God, and know my heart;
Try me and know my anxious thoughts;
And see if there be any hurtful way in me,
And lead me in the everlasting way.

—PSALM 139:23–24

Progress, Not Perfection

Read: Recovery becomes a way of life for people in Alcoholics Anonymous and other such groups. In some ways, it may become your experience as well. As you spend time working each step during the following weeks, you will learn how valuable this soul-searching process can be. As you gently open your life, exposing your wounds and your sorrows, you'll begin to experience peace and contentment—perhaps for the first time in many years.

You'll be on the road to a more rewarding life than you've ever lived—a life where wisdom and sound judgment rule rather than wishful thinking. At the same time, there will be setbacks—times when you regress to rebellious thoughts and attitudes. Your behavior may be equally poor. When this occurs, stop as quickly as you recognize what is happening, and determine where you are falling short. Figure out the problem, and work the appropriate step again. Ask a friend to help you, if needed. Repeat this process as often as necessary until you get back on track. It's okay to work it dozens of times if necessary.

Don't give up, regardless of what happens, and don't allow yourself to think all of your progress has evaporated. It hasn't; it's just a setback. Be gentle with yourself when you regress, realizing it can happen to anybody. It's like stumbling. When you fall down, you get back up, brush yourself off, and move forward. You don't say, "I've fallen down, and I'll never get up again." It's the same with recovering from an abusive situation. When you fall, get up and continue your journey.

In recovery, look for progress rather than perfection. By working on your recovery a little each day, progress is inevitable. It will occur; you can count on it. You are a work in progress; you're not perfect. Neither is anyone else. Dwell on the progress being made—not on where you still fall short. As the months and years pass, you'll be amazed by the progress you've made. Your feet will become firmly planted, strong and stable, and, in whatever you do, you'll prosper.

I say to every man among you not to think more highly of himself than he ought to think; but to think so as to have sound judgment, as God has allotted to each a measure of faith. (ROMANS 12:3)

Pray: God, enable me to truly engage in this process of recovery. Help me understand where I am in the process. Please heal me at the core of who I am—in all the tender, vulnerable areas.

Write: Give yourself permission to be "a work in progress." Take a moment to reflect on how much your attitude toward recovery has improved already. Write down three areas that need progress. Now thank God for being willing to change you.

Reflect
> *He gives strength to the weary,*
> *And to him who lacks might He increases power.*
> *Though youths grow weary and tired,*
> *And vigorous young men stumble badly,*
> *Yet those who wait for the LORD*
> *Will gain new strength;*
> *They will mount up with wings like eagles,*
> *They will run and not get tired,*
> *They will walk and not become weary.*

—ISAIAH 40:29–31

A Constant Source for Guidance

Read: As you begin the 11-step journey, there are two prayers that can be a constant source of guidance and comfort—one authored by a Protestant theologian, the other by a Catholic saint. Both epitomize the recovery mind-set perfectly.

Refer to each as often as necessary. In time, you may choose to commit both to memory. There's no downside to these prayers. Utilize them. Allow them to filter into your soul and become a part of the fabric of who you are. Both will help you when times are tough—when you want to quit, when you want to return to your old ways. The first prayer below is by the Protestant theologian.

SERENITY PRAYER—REINHOLD NIEBUHR

God,

Grant me the serenity
To accept the things I cannot change;
Courage to change the things I can;
And wisdom to know the difference.

Living one day at a time;
Enjoying one moment at a time;
Accepting hardships as the pathway to peace;

Taking, as He did, this sinful world
As it is, not as I would have it;

Trusting that He will make all things right,
If I surrender to His Will;

That I may be reasonably happy in this life
And supremely happy with Him
Forever in the next.

Amen

PURPOSEFUL PRAYER—SAINT FRANCIS OF ASSISI

Lord, make me an instrument of Your peace;
Where there is hatred, let me sow love;
Where there is injury, pardon;
Where there is doubt, faith;
Where there is despair, hope;
Where there is darkness, light; and
Where there is sadness, joy.

Grant that I may not so much seek
To be consoled, as to console;
To be understood, as to understand;
To be loved, as to love;

For it is in giving that we receive;
It is in pardoning that we are pardoned;
And it is in dying that we are born to eternal life.

As you begin your journey in recovery, know there will be times when you will want to quit. You will have difficult days. Resist the temptation to give up. Persevere. It will be worth it. Remember, every negative thought and feeling you experience during the process is already inside you—just below the surface. To move forward with your life, you must free yourself from their debilitating weight, and there's no better way to do this than to meet them head-on. That's what recovery is all about.

With this truth firmly in mind, it's time to begin the 11 steps.

Be strong and courageous! Do not tremble or be dismayed, for the
LORD your God is with you wherever you go. (JOSHUA 1:9)

Pray: Father, it will take courage to move ahead in recovery. Please give me the persevering attitude I need to move forward.

Write: Read the above prayers three times each to help you become familiar with them. Ask God to apply them to your heart. You also might decide to copy them down and post them where you can see them repeatedly—perhaps on the refrigerator door or bathroom mirror.

Reflect

We can rejoice, too, when we run into problems and trials, for we know that they help us develop endurance. And endurance develops strength of character, and character strengthens our confident hope of salvation. And this hope will not lead to disappointment. For we know how dearly God loves us, because he has given us the Holy Spirit to fill our hearts with his love.

When we were utterly helpless, Christ came at just the right time and died for us sinners.

—ROMANS 5:3–6 NLT

STEP 1

I acknowledge that my life is shipwrecked and
not where I want it to be.

Introduction

I acknowledge that my life is shipwrecked and not where I want it to be.

On the surface, step 1 may appear to be the easiest step to recovery. All you have to do is recognize your situation accurately and acknowledge it. That's simple, right?

In a sense, it is the easiest step, but for more people than not, it's by far the most difficult. That's because you have to "admit" you're not okay the way you are and that you need help. Acknowledging this truth may be very difficult.

It takes substantial time and enormous heartache to be willing to seek help. But that's what is required—seeking and accepting help. You have to admit you are not okay and will not be okay without it.

Step 1 deals with denial. Denial is the false belief—maintained steadfastly—that you have everything under control when you clearly do not. Those in denial say, "I'm fine the way I am. There's nothing wrong with me. I don't need help. Leave me alone!"

Denial can be more deceptive for those who have been religiously abused than for alcoholics or drug addicts. The reason is simple: you are never incarcerated for driving under the influence of religious abuse. Neither is there a field sobriety test for it, which makes denial much easier.

The devastation from religious abuse is primarily internal—in your heart and in your soul, where the destruction manifests itself in negative emotions and attitudes. Shame, bitterness, anger, and revenge are its fruit. Unlike the effects of alcoholism, you will not develop cirrhosis of the liver—just hard-heartedness, which can be equally detrimental to your health.

This is why it's so difficult for some to admit their life is shipwrecked. They can't see the destruction from the outside, but it's there on the inside—just below the surface.

Perhaps this is where you are right now, and you are having a moment of clarity—a moment of truth. You know you're not where you want to be. That's what step 1 is all about—changing your internal perspective. Instead of living in denial, you need to develop a state of mind that acknowledges reality and maintains this perspective throughout the process. It will do you no good to admit you need help one day and then change your mind the next. To recover, you have to work the 11 steps as vigorously as an alcoholic works his or her program of sobriety.

If you're ready to admit you have a problem, then you're ready to make some progress. You're ready for recovery.

Pruning Produces a Better Person

I acknowledge that my life is shipwrecked and not where I want it to be.

Read: When I first invited Christ into my life, I had visions about the plans God had for me. Most new converts do. Because I was young, my visions were grandiose and very self-centered, but I didn't realize it. I convinced myself they were from the Lord.

After being a Christian for many years, I remember praying, *Thank You, Lord. You've spared me from so much. Nothing difficult has ever happened to me, and I owe it all to You.* Although my prayer was heartfelt, it was also self-centered and immature. From that moment forward, things began to change, which challenged every area of my life.

I experienced heartbreak at a level I thought would destroy me. But it didn't. It made me stronger—in spite of myself. At the time, I thought my difficulties were some sort of punishment, but I was wrong. Though pain is not purposed by God, He definitely used it to prune me and to make me more fruitful. If you've ever been a gardener, you know pruning increases fruitfulness. When humans are pruned, however, it hurts—it hurts a lot.

For me, the bottom line was this: I was not where I thought I was in my walk with God—not even close. I was a little boy dressed up in a man's clothes, but nothing about me resembled a mature man in Christ. God wanted me to be an adult, and it required a great deal of pruning to make that a reality.

If you're reading this, the same is probably true for you. If it is, let God have His way, and know it will make you a better person—much better. You'll like how you turn out and so will those you love. You'll finally be who you were intended to be.

I am the true vine, and My Father is the vinedresser. Every branch in Me that does not bear fruit, He takes away; and every branch that bears fruit, He prunes it so that it may bear more fruit. (JOHN 15:1–2)

Pray: Father, I want You to have Your way with me, but much of the time, I don't know what that is. Right now—this very minute—I give myself to You. I choose to believe that the pruning You are doing in my life will make me into the person You want me to be. Please help me keep my heart and my eyes on You. I know that when I do, I will not be disappointed.

Write: It's okay to be exactly where you are. Stop pretending you're someone you're not. It doesn't work. Remember, denial is never an appropriate response in recovery. Stop making excuses about where you are in life. Instead, tell God—and yourself—precisely where you are. Write a sentence or short paragraph describing your situation. Be completely honest.

You can't be where you aren't. You'll never get out of the hole you're in until you stop digging. Invite God to join you exactly where you are. Even if it's into the darkest, foulest emotional hell on earth, He will come. When you've done that, thank Him for everything He intends to do to make you into the person He wants you to be. Remember, God's fruit is love, joy, peace, patience, kindness, gentleness, faithfulness, goodness, and self-control.

Reflect

Many are the afflictions of the righteous;
But the LORD delivers him out of them all.

—PSALM 34:19

Those who plant in tears
  will harvest with shouts of joy.
They weep as they go to plant their seed,
  but they sing as they return with the harvest.

—PSALM 126:5–6 NLT

Rich in the World's Eyes

I acknowledge that my life is shipwrecked and not where I want it to be.

Read: When I received Christ as my Lord and Savior as a nineteen-year-old, I was told, "God has a wonderful plan for your life." In my mind, this statement equated to power, success, prestige, and wealth. Because I was eager for these things, I readily accepted the invitation.

Looking back years later, those initial words seem more like a well-oiled sales pitch than anything else. My life has not been what I anticipated—not in a materialistic way. That's probably true of you as well.

What I thought God had in store for me wasn't even close to what has happened. I wanted to be rich in the world's eyes; He wanted me to be rich in character. I wanted to be admired; He wanted me to be trustworthy. I wanted to be knowledgeable; He wanted me to be wise.

Need I tell you who won this battle of the wills?

He did, of course, as He always does—as He should. What I have learned during the journey, however, has made me a much better man than I ever dreamed possible.

So here's my encouragement to you: let the Lord have His way, and He will make you into a person worth knowing. He's going to have His way regardless, so learn to enjoy the process rather than fight it. It will make your life much more rewarding.

You will make known to me the path of life; In Your presence is fullness of joy; In Your right hand there are pleasures forever. (PSALM 16:11)

Pray: Lord, give me the strength to submit to Your will rather than try to live by my own. Help me to realize that Your way and Your purpose are better than mine.

Write: Where are you in life, and what is your relationship with God? Take time to journal about where you find yourself right now. Be completely honest. It's important for your recovery.

Reflect

As the heavens are higher than the earth,
So are My ways higher than your ways
And My thoughts than your thoughts.

—ISAIAH 55:9

When Dysfunction Becomes a Problem

I acknowledge that my life is shipwrecked and not where I want it to be.

Read: Throughout the Bible, we are taught to welcome strangers, clothe the naked, and give of ourselves to those in need. Jesus teaches us that what we do for the "least of these" is what we do for Him. The church is asked to be the voice for the voiceless and the defender of the afflicted. When this process works, it is beautiful to behold, but when it doesn't, dysfunction ensues—sometimes quite a bit of it.

Most of the dysfunction results from fallen humanity's behaving as such. Sometimes it's much worse than that. This is when abusiveness becomes a problem. Because many Christians are young and naive, they accept beliefs that contradict God's principles. When they ask their trusted leaders to explain what's happening, the explanations often contradict biblical teaching. Does this sound familiar?

When this happens, you should run. At some level, you know this is what you need to do, but that's not what happened, is it? Instead you "resold yourself" about what was occurring, making the contradiction a cherished belief instead of what it was—a destructive error. That's where the problem began.

Those who don't know the Scriptures make easy targets for abusive leaders. Such leaders know the Bible well enough to distort it. For this reason, it's easy to abuse young, trusting people who are poorly grounded. The end results are shipwrecked lives. Has this been your experience? If so, you're not alone.

Recovering from a situation where you completely trusted a misguided authority figure is very difficult. Your soul is seared with scar tissue cover-

48

ing the wound, and you become skeptical and jaded for a long time—sometimes years.

If this is where you are, acknowledge it. By recognizing and admitting this reality rather than denying it, you are taking a critical step in your recovery.

Your word is a lamp to guide my feet and a light for my path. (PSALM 119:105 NLT)

Pray: Lord, help me recognize where I am in my spiritual and emotional life. Give me the courage to be honest with myself and with You about this—consistently honest.

Write: Take time to consider where you are in your spiritual, emotional, and physical life. Write it down. If you are not someone who likes to journal, confide in a safe friend. But remember, your recovery depends on being completely forthright—and by all means, make sure your confidant is truly safe.

Reflect
> *As the rain and the snow come down from heaven,*
>> *And do not return there without watering the earth*
>> *And making it bear and sprout,*
>> *And furnishing seed to the sower and bread to the eater;*
> *So will My word be which goes forth from My mouth;*
>> *It will not return to Me empty,*
>> *Without accomplishing what I desire,*
>> *And without succeeding in the matter for which I sent it.*
>> —ISAIAH 55:10–11

The Power of Denial

I acknowledge that my life is shipwrecked and not where I want it to be.

Read: Few things are as difficult as the time following religious abuse. After the initial shock, which can last anywhere from a few days to several months, a wave of bitterness overcomes you. Then it remains until you make a conscious decision to refuse to allow it to rule your life.

Most people go to elaborate lengths to convince others they are not bitter. Worst of all, they also try to convince themselves they are not bitter—usually with a great deal of success. No recovery is possible as long as you are in this mental state. If you're bitter, you have to come clean about it.

By the way, many people have learned to control their emotions masterfully. Perhaps you responded calmly on the outside but were offended and enraged on the inside? When it comes to bitterness and denial, your emotional state on the inside is the only true barometer—not what you show to others on the outside.

Take a moment before God to become honest with yourself—completely honest. It's required before any healing can begin. Without soul-searching honesty, you'll never start the healing process. It's not possible.

> *Behold, You desire truth in the innermost being,*
> *And in the hidden part You will make me know wisdom.* (PSALM 51:6)

Pray: God, give me the courage to face the truth. I need Your strength to face all that is going on inside of me.

Write: Take a minute to look back and reflect upon your abuse. When you do, answer the following questions:

- Has anyone ever told you how bitter you are?
- If so, how did you respond?
- Did you admit the truth, or did you deny it?
- Did it make you angry? If so, how angry were you?

Be honest; this is a great measuring stick.

Reflect

The LORD is righteous in all His ways
    And kind in all His deeds.
The LORD is near to all who call upon Him,
    To all who call upon Him in truth.
He will fulfill the desire of those who fear Him;
    He will also hear their cry and will save them.

—PSALM 145:17–19

Injured Relationships

I acknowledge that my life is shipwrecked and not where I want it to be.

Read: *We must never allow anything to injure our relationship with God. If it does get injured, we must take time to put it right* (Oswald Chambers).

I don't think it's possible to go through an experience of religious abuse without injuring your relationship with God. It just goes with the territory.

The tendency for those who have been religiously abused is to sweep the problem under the rug and proceed with life—as if nothing has happened. This is a mistake, but it's one most people make. It's difficult to deal with the anger and pain associated with religious abuse; but if you don't go through it, you will never learn the lesson you're required to learn, and you'll probably be destined to be abused again.

That's the value of recovery. Regardless of which part of the problem is yours, you don't have to live with the consequences any longer. You can recover and be a better person for the experience.

As far as the east is from the west,
So far has He removed our transgressions from us. (PSALM 103:12)

Pray: Lord, please show me the ways I have injured my relationship with You and others. Forgive me and help me to forgive myself. Help me to simply release it and become the person You want me to be.

Write: On a sheet of paper, describe the ways you have hurt yourself and others. Prayerfully discuss this list with God. Then write across the paper:

Step 1

If we confess our sins, He is faithful and righteous to forgive us our sins and to cleanse us from all unrighteousness. (1 JOHN 1:9)

Once you have written this verse across the paper, tear up the list and throw it away. You are forgiven.

Reflect

Though I walk in the midst of trouble, You will revive me;
  You will stretch forth Your hand against the wrath of my enemies,
  And Your right hand will save me.

—PSALM 138:7

The LORD is good,
  A stronghold in the day of trouble,
  And He knows those who take refuge in Him.

—NAHUM 1:7

It's Abuse—Plain and Simple

I acknowledge that my life is shipwrecked and not where I want it to be.

Read: Long-suffering, which is also known as patience, is a fruit of the Spirit of God. It seems to be the one loved by abusive people the most. They don't practice it themselves; that's not their style. But they do require it of you. It's one of the ways they control you. It's how they manipulate you into validating their unacceptable behavior. As they impose their will on you, which you know intuitively to be wrong, they tell you that good Christians practice patience and long-suffering. To justify aberrant behavior, they tell you that the ends justify the means. Accepting their abuse with grace and long-suffering, they tell you, is your duty—your responsibility. If you don't, you're chided for being spiritually immature.

Does this sound familiar?

If it does, you're not alone. It happens frequently, but this is not what long-suffering is—not even close. If you submit to what is wrong and call it right, your life will become shipwrecked. It's abuse—plain and simple. This robs you in every way—emotionally, financially, and morally. Remember, there's no right way to do a wrong thing—regardless of how persuasive your abuser may be.

When long-suffering comes from God, it builds your character, establishes you as a person of faith, and allows you to grow spiritually. It makes difficulties something you endure with grace, and it often points someone, who observes your situation, to Christ. It's the best form of witnessing there is; nothing compares to it. When it's counterfeited, however, it's destructive and does great harm to you personally.

How can you tell the difference between the two? Compare the reality of what's happening with what the Scriptures teach. If what is happening doesn't jibe with what the Scriptures teach, it's wrong and nothing can make it right. Worst of all, it's like an emotional cul-de-sac. The further you journey in, the longer it takes to get back on the right road.

> *The Holy Spirit produces this kind of fruit in our lives: love, joy, peace, patience, kindness, goodness, faithfulness, gentleness, and self-control. There is no law against these things!* (GALATIANS 5:22–23 NLT)

Pray: Lord, I don't want to keep spinning round and round, getting nowhere. Heal me and lead me by Your hand to truth and wisdom.

Write: Ask yourself today and journal about the following questions:

- In which areas of my life have I been broken, confused, and abused?
- In which areas do I want to be different?
- What would this look like?
- What is my next step to making these changes happen?

Reflect
Remember the word to Your servant,
In which You have made me hope.
This is my comfort in my affliction,
That Your word has revived me.
The arrogant utterly deride me,
Yet I do not turn aside from Your law.

—PSALM 119:49–51

WEEK 3

STEP 2

I commit to stop living my life in pursuit of
self-defeating behavior.

Introduction

I commit to stop living my life in pursuit of self-defeating behavior.

When you've been abused, the damage burrows deep inside you—to the tender, most vulnerable places. It seems as if the air is taken right out of you—as well as your joy for life. It defeats and debilitates every aspect of your being, producing discouragement, disillusionment, and depression. Low self-esteem overwhelms you as you experience feelings of shame and worthlessness. Instead of being confident, resilient, and open, you retreat into a world of fear, becoming indecisive and tenuous—a shadow of who you used to be. Abuse devalues you in every area of your life, which is precisely what your abuser intended.

When I was a kid, I heard this rhyme all the time:

Sticks and stones
May break my bones,
But names can never hurt me.

You remember it, don't you? Whenever someone called me a name, I would repeat it and believed it was true.

As I've thought about the rhyme as an adult, however, my perspective has changed. Broken bones heal and, over time, become a distant memory. Names, on the other hand, burrow deep inside you. Some cast a shaming imprint, which changes you for a lifetime. Without help, you may never recover—not completely anyway.

That's the worst part of religious abuse. It's a pronouncement that you are unworthy—not up to par, that there's something fundamentally wrong with you. Your very best isn't good enough, so why try?

When you feel this way about yourself, self-defeating actions invariably follow suit. That's why abused people turn to alcohol, drugs, pornography, promiscuity, overspending, overeating, unnecessary medications, and suicidal ideations. If you believe you are worthless, you do worthless things. Your behavior becomes self-defeating, and you turn into the person your abuser accused you of being.

By your actions, you validate their predictions, making their accusations appear to be on target. But you don't have to continue playing the game. You can stop the self-destructive cycle and become everything God intended you to be. It's possible, but you have to make the choice to do so.

To recover, you have to recognize this pattern of behavior and make a conscious commitment to abandon the "sin that so easily besets you" (see Hebrews 12:1) It's not easy, but you can do it. That's why step 2 is so important. It's an act of the will. It's standing up for yourself; it's fighting back. It's saying no to self-defeating behavior.

Tired of Self-Defeating Behavior?

I commit to stop living my life in pursuit of self-defeating behavior.

Read: After you've experienced religious abuse, life changes—not a little but substantially. Life is never the same again, no matter how fervently you desire it. It's just not possible. No matter how much you want to, you just can't return to a life of naïveté. The reason is simple: you know too much. Your eyes have been opened, and once enlightened, you can never retreat to the simplicity of your former innocence.

Because returning to an easier way of life is no longer an option, many choose to throw in the towel, abandoning God and Christianity. Although it's not always a conscious decision, abused people live half-lives—consumed with bitterness and shame. Having experienced abuse at the hands of a trusted religious leader, many refuse to become vulnerable again. Through cynicism, contempt, and anger, they harden their hearts, protecting themselves from further abuse.

They believe their self-protectiveness is beneficial, but they are mistaken. By remaining bitter, they actually validate the abuse, which holds them prisoners to their pasts and prevents them from being able to experience fruitful futures. They become stuck, unable to move emotionally or spiritually, trapped in a joyless life—a life they have chosen for themselves.

Is this where you are? If so, the good news is that there is a way out—a way to become all you were ever meant to be. God is still there for you, waiting to reestablish you in a different way. It may not be the life you dreamed of, but it's the life you were meant to live. Having been wounded, like God's Son, you can experience the abundant life promised by God when you first believed. But this time, you'll have your eyes wide open, making you more useful to yourself and to others. Although your life will be different, it will also be aligned with God's purpose for you—a purpose rich in fulfillment.

> *The thief comes only to steal and kill and destroy; I came that they may have life, and have it abundantly.* (JOHN 10:10)

Pray: Father, root out the bitterness and anger I know is inside me. Bring me back to You—back to a relationship that is intimate and full. Return a sense of peace to me, please.

Write: Reestablishing intimacy after being hurt can be very difficult. Begin by writing a list of everything that frightens you about reconnecting with God. Be thorough and honest with this list. It doesn't matter how disillusioned you have become. God will meet you right where you are—no matter how far from Him you have wandered.

Reflect

> *I waited patiently for the LORD to help me,*
>   *and he turned to me and heard my cry.*
> *He lifted me out of the pit of despair,*
>   *out of the mud and the mire.*
> *He set my feet on solid ground*
>   *and steadied me as I walked along.*
> *He has given me a new song to sing,*
>   *a hymn of praise to our God.*
> *Many will see what he has done and be amazed.*
>   *They will put their trust in the LORD.*
>
> —PSALM 40:1–3 NLT

Driving in a Cul-de-sac

I commit to stop living my life in pursuit of self-defeating behavior.

Read: Being estranged from God is like driving in a cul-de-sac. It will never get you anywhere. When you go down the road of estrangement from God, you never make any progress. All you do is travel back and forth meaninglessly, never making any progress. You'll just have to turn around and come back the way you came. It's okay to do it, but it's really a waste of time—your time!

I know what you're probably thinking. You didn't cause the problem. Your estrangement from God came because of what someone else has done—because of another's actions. It's the abuser's fault, not yours.

You feel like a victim, and you may be right. There are millions just like you—people who have been cast aside from churches and ministries—abused, abandoned, and forgotten. You would be fine—if you hadn't been exploited, humiliated, and contemptuously dismissed as a person without value.

Regardless of the situation, however, you are still responsible for your spiritual state of mind—not your abuser. Nobody can change your situation except you. You have to do it for yourself. You have to stop the self-defeating cycle.

I know you don't think it's fair, and you're right. It isn't fair, but that's the way it is. You're responsible for getting your act together and reestablishing your relationship with God. By living in a constant state of bitterness and resentment, you are only hurting yourself. You do have a purpose in life, and driving back and forth on an emotional dead-end street isn't it.

*"For I know the plans I have for you," says the LORD. "They are
plans for good and not for disaster, to give you a future and a hope."*
(JEREMIAH 29:11 NLT)

Pray: Lord, help me to stop dwelling on the past, to stop thinking about how badly I have been hurt. Help me put the past where it belongs—behind me. Teach me what I need to learn from the situation, and show me the path forward. Give me the strength I need to move ahead with my life. Give me Your strength.

Write: What are some of the dead ends in your life? Name them and write about them, or share them with a safe friend. As you do, invite God to spend time with you and illuminate your mind, showing you how to avoid them in the future.

Reflect

God called you to do good, even if it means suffering, just as Christ suffered for you. He is your example, and you must follow in his steps. He never sinned, nor ever deceived anyone.

—I PETER 2:21–22 NLT

Since Christ suffered physical pain, you must arm yourselves with the same attitude he had, and be ready to suffer, too. For if you have suffered physically for Christ, you have finished with sin. You won't spend the rest of your lives chasing your own desires, but you will be anxious to do the will of God.

—I PETER 4:1–2 NLT

God Has Heard It All

I commit to stop living my life in pursuit of self-defeating behavior.

Read: Being abused seems unreal. When it first occurs, you say to yourself, *This isn't really happening. It can't be happening—not to me.*

To most, it seems surreal, and it's nearly always unexpected. It's a violation of a person's life—of a person's soul. It's like someone is pointing a gun in your face—but not exactly. It's more like a knife that cuts your soul and leaves you bleeding emotionally—with a wound that never seems to heal completely.

Soon enough, however, every aspect of the abuse becomes clear as its crushing reality debilitates you, producing pain in every fiber of your being. Because the pain is excruciating and often unbearable, the anger that comes from it can be consuming. When it does, you lash out—often at those you love.

But that's not all. Because the abuse is unjustified, as is all abuse, you probably find yourself bitter toward God as well. You blame Him even though it hurt Him as much as it did you. In your anger, you demand:

- *Why did You allow this to happen to me?*
- *If You would allow this, I don't want anything to do with You.*
- *Christians are hypocrites. I'll never have anything to do with them again—never.*

God has heard it all—millions of times. All of these reactions are normal, but if you allow any of them to rule your life, you'll never be the person you're capable of being. You'll be half a person, living your years without purpose—unfulfilled and bitter. God doesn't want that for you, and neither do you. He wants you healed from your emotional wounds, but you have to want it as well.

You have to be an active participant in your recovery. If you're willing to go to any length to extricate yourself from the pit you're in, recovery will occur. It's inevitable. But it takes effort, sustained effort—initiated by you.

Are you ready to begin? If so, start by making a commitment to never retreat into self-defeating behavior again.

He will surely be gracious to you at the sound of your cry; when He hears it, He will answer you. (ISAIAH 30:19)

Pray: Father, give me the courage to desire recovery—to want it with all of my heart. I don't want to stay in this place, but I need Your strength to take the necessary steps to bring healing into my life.

Write: Consider God's concern for you. He is truly good and trustworthy. Think of Him as a loving parent. Take some time to journal about what He might say concerning your pain and suffering. You might write a dialogue about it.

Reflect

By his wounds
*   you are healed.*
Once you were like sheep
*   who wandered away.*
But now you have turned to your Shepherd,
*   the Guardian of your souls.*

—I PETER 2:24–25 NLT

A single day in your courts
*   is better than a thousand anywhere else!*
I would rather be a gatekeeper in the house of my God
*   than live the good life in the homes of the wicked.*
For the LORD God is our sun and our shield.
*   He gives us grace and glory.*
The LORD will withhold no good thing
*   from those who do what is right.*

—PSALM 84:10–11 NLT

Your State of Mind

I commit to stop living my life in pursuit of self-defeating behavior.

Read: *Many of us prefer to stay at the threshold of the Christian life instead of going on to construct a soul in accordance with the new life God has put within. We fail because we are ignorant of the way we are made. We put things down to the devil instead of our own undisciplined natures. Think what we can be when we are roused!* (Oswald Chambers).

The single greatest enemy to any person's recovery is his or her state of mind. Once you have been abused, you feel defeated and worthless, which is precisely the message your abuser intended you to internalize.

Although it's normal to have feelings of worthlessness as a result of abuse, it's self-defeating to embrace these feelings and make them a part of who you are. If you want to be a whole person, you must renew your mind and reject what your abuser has said about you. It isn't accurate; don't accept it as true. If you already have, make a commitment to deal with the false message consciously and consistently. It's destructive—delivered to poison your mind and your soul. Don't allow your abuser to have this power over you. Resist it at all costs.

There are three things you must do repeatedly:

1. In your thoughts, stop repeating the message said about you—the words that stung so deeply and continue to wound.

2. In your heart, make an effort to disagree with these lies. Fight against the inclination to accept them as true. Call them what they are—lies, half-truths, and distortions.

3. Internalize what God has said about you—that He loves you, has plans for you, and wants to give you a hope and a future.

The way to counteract the lie is simple, but that doesn't make it easy. It's difficult, but summoning the will to renew your mind consistently and repeatedly may be the most important thing you ever do. Over time, you will learn to reject the lies and believe the truth.

Keep in mind that this kind of self-affirmation has to be done repeatedly; it's never a one-time thing. You have to do it every day—sometimes every hour. At first, it may feel uncomfortable, but the value of making the effort is incalculable. Keep at it—even if it feels awkward. If you do, recovery will begin.

Do not be conformed to this world, but be transformed by the renewing of your mind, so that you may prove what the will of God is, that which is good and acceptable and perfect. (ROMANS 12:2)

Pray: Father, help me make my thoughts captive to Your leadership—all of my thoughts. Help me believe You love me and desire my recovery. Help me recognize that my relationship with You is sealed because of Christ's efforts and not my own.

Write: Set aside some time each day to "renew your mind." Start with five minutes a day. During this time, meditate on God's truth, especially what He says about you—that you are His dearly loved child. Tell yourself this repeatedly. It's true.

Reflect

Lord, don't hold back your tender mercies from me.
Let your unfailing love and faithfulness always protect me.
—PSALM 40:11 NLT

Brethren, whatever is true, whatever is honorable, whatever is right, whatever is pure, whatever is lovely, whatever is of good repute, if there is any excellence and if anything worthy of praise, dwell on these things.
—PHILIPPIANS 4:8

Seeking the Kingdom

I commit to stop living my life in pursuit of self-defeating behavior.

Read: *The greatest concern of our lives is not the Kingdom of God, but how we are to fit ourselves to live. Jesus reverses the order: Get rightly related to God first, maintain that as the great care of your life, and never put the concern of your care on the other things* (Oswald Chambers).

Putting the kingdom of God first can be the most difficult thing in the world to do, especially for materialistically minded Americans. For us, Christianity is fine—just as long as we can be affluent and comfortable. If our creature comforts are threatened, we rarely consider it to be God's will. *God would never want me to experience such difficulties*, we reason.

For us, prosperity and a solid economic foundation are synonymous with God's purpose for our lives. If this belief is challenged, we reject it. If a minister teaches frugality and contentment with a moderate lifestyle, we shop around until we find a church that will validate our consumptive inclinations. We erroneously equate the acquisition of material comfort with God's will.

When we are religiously abused, it can be a "blessing" in disguise. Our world is shattered—including our visions for personal prosperity—and herein lies a hidden blessing.

This means we have to look at life differently—more thoughtfully and less materialistically. We have to renew our minds to see new possibilities, which is precisely what God wants us to do. Shattered people who want their lives to be fulfilled, cease to be self-centered and begin to seek God's leading at a deeper level. Until this happens, however, it never occurs to most that God wants them to be rich in character, which has far more value to Him than a pleasant, carefree lifestyle.

Consequently, the next time you see a friend go through something horrific, especially an abusive situation, pay careful attention to what's happening. God may be at work in this person's life, bringing good out of evil. If you've been through it, you know what I mean, don't you? It's a hard experience, but the end result can be extraordinarily worthwhile.

> *Seek first His kingdom and His righteousness, and all these things will be added to you.* (MATTHEW 6:33)

Pray: Father, I know my perspective about life is very short-term. Help me see things as You see them—from an eternal perspective. Allow me to receive all of the wisdom that I need about my abusive situation.

Write: Take some time to document how you spend your time, talents, and income. As you look at your priorities, how have they changed since the abuse? Ask yourself if they need to change further. What would they look like in an ideal situation? Ask God for the grace to make the changes needed to align them with His will.

Reflect

> *I have learned how to be content with whatever I have. I know how to live on almost nothing or with everything. I have learned the secret of living in every situation, whether it is with a full stomach or empty, with plenty or little.*
>
> —PHILIPPIANS 4:11–12 NLT

> *We know that God causes all things to work together for good to those who love God, to those who are called according to His purpose.*
>
> —ROMANS 8:28

Changing Your Will

I commit to stop living my life in pursuit of self-defeating behavior.

Read: I love the V8 commercials. They say that you had the opportunity to make a good choice about what you put in your body, but you foolishly chose something that wasn't nutritious—something with empty calories. Because Americans make poor food choices repeatedly, we have weight and health issues galore.

This principle is also true spiritually. In the aftermath of religious abuse, nearly everyone makes some very poor choices—morally, mentally, and emotionally. We feel defeated, so we act as if we have been defeated—as if our value to God and to ourselves has ceased to exist. In essence, we accept as true what has been said about us, and we behave poorly as a result. Metaphorically, we eat candy and cake instead of having a V8, feeling bad about ourselves while, at the same time, looking pitiful to others.

If you want your life to count—to have meaning and purpose—you have to change this pattern of self-defeating behavior. It begins by changing your will.

Always remember this: what your abuser meant for evil, God means for good. Life is not over for you—although you may think it is. The vision of what you thought your life would be has passed, but God's vision for what He wants for you certainly has not. He still loves you; He still has a plan for your life; and He definitely wants you to be everything He created you to be.

So, as an act of your will, stop wallowing in discontent. Stop thinking and behaving like a failure. The game is not over; it may have just begun. Get up and turn your heart to the Lord. It's like having a V8. It will nourish every aspect of you—your body, your mind, and your soul.

May our Lord Jesus Christ Himself and God our Father, who has loved us and given us eternal comfort and good hope by grace, comfort and strengthen your hearts in every good work and word.
(2 THESSALONIANS 2:16–17)

Pray: Father, help me to stop behaving in a self-defeating way. Show me how to stop wallowing in the past. Help me press forward to a more fulfilling future. Give me faith to believe. I do believe just a little, but it's difficult. Help me with my unbelief.

Write: What would it look like for you to press forward and stop living in the past? Write this out. Where do you want to be emotionally, physically, and spiritually six months from now? How about one year from now? How about five years from now? Take twenty minutes to describe your hopes and aspirations. Don't get stuck in trying to "get it right." Just consider your future before God, and journal your first impressions about where you want to be. Update your evaluation as often as you desire.

Reflect

My eyes are continually toward the LORD,
For He will pluck my feet out of the net.
Turn to me and be gracious to me,
For I am lonely and afflicted.
The troubles of my heart are enlarged;
Bring me out of my distresses.

—PSALM 25:15–17

Joseph said to them, "Do not be afraid, for am I in God's place? As for you, you meant evil against me, but God meant it for good in order to bring about this present result, to preserve many people alive."

—GENESIS 50:19–20

WEEK 4

STEP 3

I accept that the responsibility for getting back on track is mine and no one else's.

Introduction

I accept that the responsibility for getting back on track is mine and no one else's.

When you get off track with God, at first it doesn't appear to be much of a detour—at least not overtly. When you become wounded and abused spiritually, you leave the Lord, as well as your abuser, behind. Throwing the baby out with the bath water feels good for a season—perhaps a long season. You're angry and you have a right to be. In your indignation, following God becomes the furthest thing from your mind.

Many have had these feelings and have abandoned their faith in God as a result. If you have done so, you're not alone. It's common when abuse occurs.

But when you turn away from God, it's like changing railroad tracks. At first, the alternate route is barely perceptible. It's just off a little. The divergence increases, however, as you speed through life going in the wrong direction—a direction that conflicts with your deepest values and beliefs.

When you finally recognize how far off track you've drifted, you start blaming others for your situation. Even if it is someone else's fault, you're still responsible for getting back on course. Blaming others doesn't solve your dilemma. It just expends your energy wastefully—purposelessly.

You have to make the decision to change directions. Nobody can do it for you. It means you have to stop, take stock of where you really are, make a plan to alter your course, and execute the plan. It can take substantial work to do so, but without it, you will never reach the destination you desire. You'll never become the person you've been created to be—rich in estimable character qualities.

Making the commitment to change course may be the most important decision you'll ever make. Without it, full recovery isn't possible, and you'll never achieve your complete potential. The alternate track never reaches

74

the place you were meant to go. Even if you're quite successful, you've missed the mark—regardless of the approbation you receive from others. Inside, where it really counts, you'll know fulfillment has eluded you.

That's why step 3 is so important. It puts the responsibility for changing direction where it belongs—on you and no one else.

God Is There—Period!

I accept that the responsibility for getting back on track is mine and no one else's.

Read: It doesn't matter whether you think God is real or not—just like it doesn't matter whether you think the world is round or flat. God's existence doesn't depend upon your opinion—whether positive or negative. Neither does the shape of the world. Your opinion has no relevance to reality.

At the same time, you might say, "But I don't 'feel' God's presence like I used to. It doesn't seem like He's paying attention to my needs."

How you feel about God is just that—your feelings—nothing more. Who He is does not depend on how you feel about Him, which should be liberating. He is there for you, regardless of the circumstance—even when it appears He couldn't care less about your situation. Regardless of your state of mind, you can count on the fact that God has not abandoned you, and your feelings will not change that reality.

Nothing can alter His commitment to you—neither life nor death, neither wealth nor poverty, neither felicity nor dysfunction. God is there—no matter what. If the quality of your relationship with Him depends on your emotional state, your blood-sugar levels will frequently be more important than His promises. Your life will be on a never-ending roller-coaster ride to nowhere—with your feelings either lifting you up or bringing you down, imprisoning you to a life of little consequence.

God is there; you can be certain of it. You can count on it—and should count on it. You can believe it because it's true—not because of anything you've done but because of what Christ has done for you. That's the reality you should never abandon or allow anyone to take from you. It doesn't matter how you feel. God is there, and His love for you has not diminished in the slightest—no matter what you've done. Neither has

His commitment. Learn to count on God's presence as a reality, not as a feeling.

I am with you always, even to the end of the age. (MATTHEW 28:20)

Pray: Lord, give me the faith to believe You are there—even when I don't feel it. When my emotions fluctuate, help me see life from Your perspective, and remind me of Your promise to never leave me or forsake me. I believe. Help me with everything that feeds into my uncertainty.

Write: Go to God with your feelings, and tell Him how you feel—*exactly how you feel.* What three adjectives describe your feelings best? Write these words on a piece of paper.

Although you should not be led by your feelings, they are real and need to be dealt with, or they will deal with you in unpleasant ways. Open your soul to God in your woundedness, and allow Him to meet you where you are. He is there, and He wants you to turn to Him with everything—even your unbelief.

Reflect
I can never escape from your Spirit!
I can never get away from your presence!
If I go up to heaven, you are there;
if I go down to the grave, you are there.
If I ride the wings of the morning,
if I dwell by the farthest oceans,
even there your hand will guide me,
and your strength will support me.

—PSALM 139:7–10 NLT

Repairing Your Relationship with God

I accept that the responsibility for getting back on track is mine and no one else's.

Read: *We must never allow anything to injure our relationship with God. If it does get injured, we must take time to put it right* (Oswald Chambers).

Like any relationship of value, your relationship with God requires time and effort to repair when it becomes injured. Due to the great pain and hurt associated with religious abuse, most choose to sweep this problem under the rug rather than deal with it. This is particularly true where God is concerned.

Avoiding spiritual problems doesn't work; it leads to self-defeating behavior. Ignoring the matter causes difficulties in nearly every area of life—often leading to significant problems like alcoholism, drug addiction, pornography, promiscuity, and obesity. Each is a desperate and destructive attempt to medicate the emotional pain associated with abuse.

Neither does it work to recite flowery prayers that you don't believe. Pretentiousness doesn't impress God. He desires intimacy, not disingenuous platitudes. If you've offended your spouse, you can't make a shallow apology and expect everything to be okay. It's the same with God. If there's a problem, you need to own up to it and make it right. God's grace is all-sufficient, but it certainly isn't cheap. Do the work necessary to make the relationship right. When you've finished, the reward will be worth the effort many times over—guaranteed.

If we confess our sins, He is faithful and righteous to forgive us our sins and to cleanse us from all unrighteousness. (1 JOHN 1:9)

Pray: Lord, show me where my relationship with You needs work. Help me be open to where I have been wrong. Forgive me for the injuries I have caused, and allow me to set things straight. Give me the strength to forsake my bitterness and turn back to You.

Write: Take the time necessary to be still before God. Ask Him how you have fallen short. Turn to the cross, take stock, and begin to make appropriate changes in your life. Be reflective and honest before God. Write a list of your shortcomings, and take them to the Lord. It's safe, because Christ has already died for every sin you've ever committed or will ever commit.

Reflect

God was fulfilling what all the prophets had foretold about the Messiah—that he must suffer these things. Now repent of your sins and turn to God, so that your sins may be wiped away. Then times of refreshment will come from the presence of the Lord.

—ACTS 3:18–20 NLT

Who God Really Is

I accept that the responsibility for getting back on track is mine and no one else's.

Read: *The purpose of God is not to answer our prayers, but by our prayers we come to discern the mind of God* (Oswald Chambers).

Idol worship was a major problem in ancient Rome. Throughout the empire, people had their personal gods, which they put on the hearth or carried in their robes wherever they went. When the Roman Empire became Christianized, they simply renamed their idols, giving them Christian names in an effort to legitimize them before God, which it certainly did not. They were still idols and had nothing to do with God—not as He has revealed Himself in the Scriptures.

In America, we have a similar problem today. We want God in our lives but on *our* terms, not His. We want the god of our understanding, not the God of the Bible. We prefer a god whose characteristics we customize to meet our specific needs. We want our god to be whatever we want him or her to be and against everything we're against. We want him to be our father, mother, the universe, our higher power, the man upstairs, or whatever else we might like. And we think God understands and accepts everything as legitimate.

Does this sound familiar? It should. This is the politically correct god of America's civil religion.

There's only one problem: this view contradicts the biblical version and our Judeo-Christian heritage. This is the place where we need to renew our minds. God is knowable—on His terms, not ours. It doesn't matter what we think God is like, but it does matter that our beliefs about God gel with what the Scriptures teach. If your beliefs line up, keep them. If they don't, read the Bible and discover who God really is. As you do, you'll be renewing your mind and transforming your life. It's also where true recovery begins, especially recovery from religious abuse. Truth sets you free. Misconception will impede your growth.

God is Light, and in Him there is no darkness at all. (1 JOHN 1:5)

Pray: Lord, help me learn who You really are—rather than who I want You to be. Thank You that You want me to know You in truth, not in pretense.

Write: Take some time to journal what you believe about God, making certain to be completely forthright. As you review what you've written, ask God to lead you to a true understanding of who He is. We can't know everything about God, but what we do know should be true. Keep your journal, and review it in one year to see how much your understanding has changed.

Reflect
> *God is the King of all the earth;*
> *Sing praises with a skillful psalm.*
> *God reigns over the nations,*
> *God sits on His holy throne.*
>
> —PSALM 47:7–8

> *You, O Lord, are a God merciful and gracious,*
> *Slow to anger and abundant in lovingkindness and truth.*
>
> —PSALM 86:15

Blaming Someone Else

I accept that the responsibility for getting back on track is mine and no one else's.

Read: When you've experienced abuse of any kind, you inevitably lose your ability to trust. Some people never retrieve it and lead half-lives that are ruled by suspicion.

If your abuse has come from a spiritual leader, you may struggle in your ability to trust God as well. Although the abuser will have to answer to God for creating the problem, it's still your responsibility to get back to the place where you began, trusting God with your life. It's easy to blame someone for your situation, but that doesn't solve the problem. You have to learn to trust again, which may be a scary thought for you.

Being in this situation is obviously very difficult, but the alternative is even worse. Once you've experienced the love of God, it's hard to settle for anything less. And chomping at the bit does nothing but waste precious years—your years, not your abuser's. Regardless of how difficult it is, you must learn to trust God once again.

> *Give thanks to the LORD, for he is good!*
> *His faithful love endures forever.* (PSALM 118:29 NLT)

Pray: Lord, I'm weary of living a half-life, and my ability to trust You is tenuous at best. I need You to restore that ability. Help me, please. I want to trust You again, but I need Your tender, healing hand to lead me.

Write: Why not make the commitment to return to your first love—a commitment to return to the Lord? Write your heavenly Father a letter, telling Him you want to get back on track with Him.

Reflect

> *Trust in the L*ORD *with all your heart,*
>   *And do not lean on your own understanding.*
> *In all your ways acknowledge Him,*
>   *And He will make your paths straight.*

—PROVERBS 3:5–6

Crisis Always Produces Change

I accept that the responsibility for getting back on track is mine and no one else's.

Read: When you experience something very difficult in life—like religious abuse, divorce, personal betrayal, or perhaps even the loss of a child, you come to an important crossroads. Your relationship with God will either become more important to you or less, but it will never remain the same. It can't. Crisis always produces change. Whether growth comes from the change, however, is something you choose.

When you're in that difficult place, God definitely has your attention— either positively or negatively. How you process the crisis is your choice. If you choose to be angry and bitter toward God because of the situation, you will have to deal with the pain in your own way. That's why so many become addicted to alcohol, drugs, pornography, prescription medications, toxic relationships, or food. Each provides comfort for a while, but none works for long. In the end, you'll have another problem to deal with and no answers to the original one. Instead you'll have another layer of debilitation.

Because you didn't learn the lesson the first time, you'll have to go through another crisis until you do—that is, if you want to grow up. There's no getting around it.

For years, I've said *Groundhog Day* is the most philosophical movie of all time. If you don't get it right the first time, you have to repeat it until you do—just like Bill Murray did in the movie. Once the lesson is learned, you become wiser and more mature. Yet if you refuse the lesson, you'll continue to remain immature in that area for the rest of your life.

That's why people become complacent in their maturity. They refuse to break through to a higher level, choosing instead to remain stuck, to remain immature. It can be scary to make the transition, but the alternative is to stunt your growth and never be all you're capable of being.

Concerning your own life, what do you choose to do? The decision—as always—is yours. So are the consequences.

> *To Him who is able to do far more abundantly beyond all that we ask or think, according to the power that works within us.*
> (EPHESIANS 3:20)

Pray: Father, give me the courage to face what is happening in my life, and enable me to gain wisdom from it. Help me learn from my mistakes, so I don't have to repeat them. Help me become everything You ever intended me to be.

Write: Take time to reflect on what has been happening in your life. What areas have you refused to face? Journal about them, or talk to a trusted friend. Running away from reality never works, so avoid denial at all costs.

Reflect

> *Even when I walk*
> *through the darkest valley,*
> *I will not be afraid,*
> *for you are close beside me.*
> *Your rod and your staff*
> *protect and comfort me.*
> *You prepare a feast for me*
> *in the presence of my enemies.*
> *You honor me by anointing my head with oil.*
> *My cup overflows with blessings.*
>
> —PSALM 23:4–5 NLT

> *The LORD also will be a stronghold for the oppressed,*
> *A stronghold in times of trouble;*
> *And those who know Your name will put their trust in You,*
> *For You, O LORD, have not forsaken those who seek You.*
>
> —PSALM 9:9–10

Are You Talking to God or Talking Back?

I accept that the responsibility for getting back on track is mine and no one else's.

Read: When you've had the rug pulled out from under you, as most of us have at one time or another, you start asking tough but important questions:

- Why did this happen?
- What does God expect from me?
- Is He really in charge of my life?
- Does He care what happens to me?
- Why have my prayers remained unanswered?

When you reach this point—and not before—God can finally have His way with you. It wasn't possible before. You had too many goals of your own to achieve. Your purpose was self-fulfillment, not abandonment to God's purpose.

When we began our walk with the Lord, we were sure He had noble, wonderful things in store for us. Failure was not a part of His plan. We didn't count on the fact that He sees life differently than we do and knows us better than we know ourselves.

He wants a relationship with us—an intimate one. He is not interested in a superficial connection, where He fulfills every request we make of Him as if He is an indulgent parent, spoiling us in the process. He wants strong men and women, not petulant kids who demand their way about everything, throwing tantrums when their demands are refused.

If you have been knocked off your feet, it might be exactly what you needed. God has a substantial investment in you, and He pays careful attention to each of His children.

Remember, you do not belong to yourself. You belong to God. With this in mind, you might start talking to God rather than talking back to Him.

As the heavens are higher than the earth,
So are My ways higher than your ways
And My thoughts than your thoughts. (ISAIAH 55:9)

Pray: Father, it's so difficult to see things from Your perspective and believe You are with me through all that is happening to me. Give me the faith to believe You are good—in spite of my circumstances. The Scriptures say You will use everything for my good. Help me accept this as the truth—as a promise.

Write: Continue to set time aside regularly to talk to God—not demanding things from Him, but getting to know Him. Renew your commitment to spend five minutes a day in spiritual reflection, and journal what God shows you. Interact with God as a dearly loved child of the King, because that is who you are.

Reflect

We know that God causes all things to work together for good to those who love God, to those who are called according to His purpose.

—ROMANS 8:28

WEEK 5

STEP 4

I choose to believe what God says about Himself:
that He is good and can be trusted.
I recognize that God is not the abuser;
rather, people who misuse their authority
are the abusers.

Introduction

I choose to believe what God says about Himself: that He is good and can be trusted. I recognize that God is not the abuser; rather, people who misuse their authority are the abusers.

Perhaps the most difficult aspect of recovery is separating God from the abuse. When abuse occurs, you're shocked, wounded, disoriented, and offended. Within a short period of time, this offense is extended to God. It's almost inevitable. In righteous indignation, you rail against Him:

- How could You let this happen to me?
- I didn't deserve this.
- This isn't fair, and You're responsible for it.
- I trusted You, and You let me down.
- I'll never trust You again—never!

Because your pain is so acute, reality is obscured, and anger toward God seems justified—even warranted. When this happens, however, you are allowing your emotions to distort reality and cloud your judgment.

By blaming God, you deprive yourself of your most valuable asset in your recovery. Additionally, you will never heal emotionally without Him. At the very best, you'll be a limited, marginal person—like a car being driven on flat tires. You're able to move forward but not at a normal, healthy pace.

You'll never find full recovery without repairing and maintaining this essential relationship.

Take a moment and reevaluate your thinking. Christ suffered abuse by religious leaders who lied about Him—just like your abusers lied about you. He was also humiliated, tortured, and murdered. More important,

He was innocent—completely innocent—when He endured mistreatment at the hands of others. He didn't deserve it—not any of it.

Now let me ask you this: Who can better understand abuse than someone who has also been abused? Who can understand being treated unfairly more than Jesus?

That is why the Lord can empathize with you so easily. He suffered as an innocent man, which allows Him to understand your woundedness, your betrayal, your frustration, and your despair. He feels your pain and loves you exactly the way you are—regardless of the circumstances.

If you want to become whole, you need to make a conscious decision to believe what God says about Himself. He loves you, and He wants your life to have value and purpose. He did not abuse you, and He definitely is not pleased with those who did.

As you think about step 4 this week, make a determined effort to separate God from the abuse. He is not responsible for it. He did not cause it—not any of it. Accepting this perspective as true is your best way to achieve full recovery, and it's the specific purpose for step 4.

Flawed Thinking Prevents Recovery

I choose to believe what God says about Himself: that He is good and can be trusted. I recognize that God is not the abuser; rather, people who misuse their authority are the abusers.

Read: Nearly every recovery program is based upon the premise that you must turn your will and your life over to the care of God—as you understand Him. Although this method works quite well for recovery from alcoholism or drug addiction, it does not work well for recovery from religious abuse. The reason is simple: In substance abuse, group consciousness often becomes the Higher Power for many, and there is only one sin—drinking or drugging.

To recover from religious abuse, however, an entirely different mind-set must be utilized. It's based on an accurate understanding of who God really is, as opposed to what you have been taught by an abusive leader. The abuser's perverted belief usually twists God's character in a way that justifies the abusive behavior.

To recover, you must know the true God as He has revealed Himself in the Scriptures, not as you project Him to be. If your understanding of God is not accurate, there is no way to recover from religious abuse. Your thinking is flawed. It just will not work. Flawed thinking is flawed thinking. If you want to be a whole person who is useful and valued by the people in your life, you must take seriously what Christ says about Himself in the Scriptures: "I am the way, and the truth, and the life; no one comes to the Father but through Me" (John 14:6).

If you take Jesus' statement at face value, as it was meant to be taken, you will never again be "ripped off" by a cult or by false teaching that makes Christ a hybrid of who He really is. This realization is particularly important for anyone who has been victimized by false teaching.

Remember, when your beliefs about God are false, the only way to ensure your recovery is to believe what is accurate. Your surest path to truth is to believe what Christ said about Himself and not what anyone else says about Him. If you do this, you will recover sooner or later. If you don't, you'll never become who God intended you to be—never. It's not possible.

If you had really known me, you would know who my Father is. From now on, you do know him and have seen him! (JOHN 14:7)

Pray: Father, reveal to me who You really are, and help me discern who You are not. Give me the faith and courage to believe that what You have said about Yourself is true. Help me discern truth from error.

Write: Consider what you think about God—who He really is. Write it out, and be honest with yourself. Answer these questions:

1. Who do I think He is?

2. What do I think He is like?

3. Have I made God into my image or the image of those around me?

When you spell this out completely, ask God to remove every misconception you have about Him and lead you to scriptural truth.

Reflect

No one has ever seen God. But the unique One, who is himself God, is near to the Father's heart. He has revealed God to us.

—JOHN 1:18 NLT

He made Him who knew no sin to be sin on our behalf, so that we might become the righteousness of God in Him.

—2 CORINTHIANS 5:21

God Wants a Relationship

I choose to believe what God says about Himself: that He is good and can be trusted. I recognize that God is not the abuser; rather, people who misuse their authority are the abusers.

Read: If being scolded, maligned, or ridiculed by someone has driven you out of your church or away from your friends, you probably think God has lost interest in you as well. That's certainly the message you received from your abuser, isn't it?

The message was crystal clear:

- The church would be better off without you.
- The church is for good people, people who don't ask questions and cause trouble.
- The church is for people who don't rock the boat—*not for people like you.*

If this is the message you received—either stated or implied—here's some really good news: God *does* want you back. In fact, He's never left your side. His love for you is unconditional. When everything in your life fails, God loves you. You may know this intuitively, or you may believe God doesn't love you because you've stopped loving yourself. But God's love has neither ceased nor diminished, regardless of the circumstances. It doesn't matter what you may or may not have done. God still loves you. He loved you when the problem occurred, and He loves you now. Nothing will ever change that.

And here's the best news of all: He wants a relationship with you—regardless of what's happened. There is a way out. There is a way through all the heartache, and it's available to you right now.

All you have to do is receive it. Are you willing to do that? If so, there's hope for you—real hope. There's also a rewarding future.

No power in the sky above or in the earth below—indeed, nothing in all creation will ever be able to separate us from the love of God that is revealed in Christ Jesus our Lord. (ROMANS 8:39 NLT)

Pray: Lord God, I need Your help, and I need it now. By faith, I accept that You love me still. This is hard for me, so please help me with my apprehension. There's an ache in my heart, and I'm very fragile. Please show me the way, Your way.

Write: Take just one step toward God today, and see what happens. Choose an action you are comfortable with. Write God a letter, talk to Him, read a verse in His Word, or go on a walk with Him. It doesn't matter what you do; just do something that moves you in His direction. Take one step toward God, and expect results to follow. If you do, the next step will be easier.

Reflect

By this the love of God was manifested in us, that God has sent His only begotten Son into the world so that we might live through Him.
—I JOHN 4:9

God, being rich in mercy, because of His great love with which He loved us, even when we were dead in our transgressions, made us alive together with Christ (by grace you have been saved), and raised us up with Him, and seated us with Him in the heavenly places in Christ Jesus, so that in the ages to come He might show the surpassing riches of His grace in kindness toward us in Christ Jesus.
—EPHESIANS 2:4–7

When Fear Consumes You

I choose to believe what God says about Himself: that He is good and can be trusted. I recognize that God is not the abuser; rather, people who misuse their authority are the abusers.

Read: One of the most prevalent emotions in the aftermath of abuse is dread—a cold fear and chilling apprehension of the future. When your world comes crashing down around you and there's nothing you can do to prevent it, anxiety inevitably overwhelms you.

Instead of looking to God for your strength, fear consumes you. You abandon your robust, positive outlook on life and shrink into a corner, becoming a nonentity—even to yourself. For you, God is nowhere to be found. It's as if He doesn't even exist. You feel alone—without value or purpose, dreading the future.

When this happens—and it's inevitable that it will—you have two choices. You can embrace your fears and become a timid, dispirited, wounded person for years—perhaps for a lifetime—or you can reject your dread and believe what God has said to be true.

In slander, betrayal, tribulation, or whatever else has decimated you, God promises to never leave you or forsake you. Think about it:

- This is either true, or it isn't.
- God is either capable of keeping His promises, or He isn't.
- He either has a future planned for you, a future with purpose, or He doesn't.

There's no in-between. Can you believe what God says about Himself: that you can count on Him regardless of what happens? Is this really true? Is God greater than your problems or not? Are His promises real or just sentimental slogans?

The choice is yours: either empower your fears or empower Almighty

God. If you choose to believe Him, your battle will still be uphill, but the conclusion is assured. You can take it to the bank; God keeps His promises.

I hold you by your right hand. . . . And I say to you, "Don't be afraid. I am here to help you." (ISAIAH 41:13 NLT)

Pray: God, I feel disconnected and abandoned concerning the events surrounding my abuse. I hurt, Father; every fiber of my being hurts. Will You meet me at the depth of my sorrow and pain where my heart is broken and my soul aches? Will You please bring healing into my life? Thank You for being safe. I know I can trust You.

Write: Consider what area in your life you are struggling with. If you don't trust God, *tell Him.* Be honest—He can take it. Write down exactly how you feel. Don't hold back. Again, make a list, if necessary. Honesty and open communication with God are critical to recovery.

Reflect

Humble yourselves under the mighty hand of God, that He may exalt you at the proper time, casting all your anxiety on Him, because He cares for you.

—1 PETER 5:6–7

Seeing that His divine power has granted to us everything pertaining to life and godliness, through the true knowledge of Him who called us by His own glory and excellence. For by these He has granted to us His precious and magnificent promises, so that by them you may become partakers of the divine nature, having escaped the corruption that is in the world by lust.

—2 PETER 1:3–4

The Lord is not slow about His promise, as some count slowness, but is patient toward you, not wishing for any to perish but for all to come to repentance.

—2 PETER 3:9

Not a Cosmic Blessing Machine

I choose to believe what God says about Himself: that He is good and can be trusted. I recognize that God is not the abuser; rather, people who misuse their authority are the abusers.

Read: In spite of what anyone might tell you, God is not a blessing machine—ready to dispense material favors upon all who ask. To think of Him in this way is nonsense, without historical or biblical foundation. When you look at the fruit of the Spirit, materialism is never mentioned. What is mentioned are love, joy, peace, patience, kindness, goodness, and other praiseworthy character qualities. Affluence isn't on the list.

Too often, most of us whine and moan because we want material things, without even the slightest consideration of whether or not receiving them is actually good for us. What we're after is a celestial bailout to help us avoid the natural consequences of our behavior.

We're like a three-year-old who cries for candy that will destroy his or her appetite for nutritional food. Because we don't understand the larger picture, which is God's purpose, we demand our way and blame Him for not answering our petulant, self-serving prayers.

He does answer our prayers but rarely in the precise way we want or expect. When prayer seems unanswered and we don't get "the stuff" we want from God, it's usually because God is working on the fruit of the Spirit in us, which He does want for us.

When you pray, what percentage of your prayer time is spent asking for something other than creature comforts? If you're like most, it's far less time than appropriate.

The thief comes only to steal and kill and destroy; I came that they may have life, and have it abundantly. (JOHN 10:10)

Pray: Lord, I know my heart. Often I want things more than I want You. I'm so sorry. Give me a deeper understanding of life. Teach me to be patient so that when everything doesn't go the way I want, I know You're still in charge and have a plan for my life—a plan for good things and not bad.

Write: Give God the benefit of the doubt. If your prayers don't result in exactly what you want, trust in His character rather than your circumstances. Make a list of character qualities you lack, and pray for God to enrich your character.

Reflect

> *Everyone who asks receives, and he who seeks finds, and to him who knocks it will be opened. Or what man is there among you who, when his son asks for a loaf, will give him a stone? Or if he asks for a fish, he will not give him a snake, will he? If you then, being evil, know how to give good gifts to your children, how much more will your Father who is in heaven give what is good to those who ask Him!*
>
> —MATTHEW 7:8–11

It Doesn't Have to Be

I choose to believe what God says about Himself: that He is good and can be trusted. I recognize that God is not the abuser; rather, people who misuse their authority are the abusers.

Read: For most people, after being subjected to a pattern of verbal and emotional abuse—and perhaps physical, sexual, or financial abuse as well—life never really returns to normalcy. Deep emotional scars can cripple abused people so badly that their lives never regain the richness they once possessed. For them, even their best days have pain and sadness.

If this is where you have been for months or years, you don't have to remain there. It doesn't have to be this way, and it most definitely is not God's will or desire for you. God loves you just the way you are—in your brokenness, in your despair, in your uncertainty. He has not given you a spirit of fear. That comes from being abused, not from Him.

He has given you a spirit of love, of power, and of discipline (see 2 Timothy 1:7). It's there just below the surface of your troubled heart, waiting for you to do the work necessary to appropriate the inner power that rightfully belongs to you—just as it does to all His children.

It's not easy regaining your composure after experiencing the deep wounds from abuse, but if you do the work necessary to heal, you will not just be as good as you once were. You'll be better—perhaps much better.

You have not received a spirit that makes you fearful slaves. Instead, you received God's Spirit when he adopted you as his own children. Now we call him, "Abba, Father." (ROMANS 8:15 NLT)

Pray: Lord, I have so much pain in my life—so much fear and sadness. I want to give it to You right now. Please take it from me, and exchange it for a spirit of love, of power, and of discipline. Heal me where I need to be healed—at the core of my being.

Write: Emotional healing takes place in different ways for different people. What has God used to heal you in the past? Is there something you can learn from this observation? What steps can you take to further your healing? Write them down, and review them whenever needed.

Reflect

I remind you to kindle afresh the gift of God which is in you through the laying on of my hands. For God has not given us a spirit of timidity, but of power and love and discipline.

—2 TIMOTHY 1:6–7

He who believes in Me, as the Scripture said, "From his innermost being will flow rivers of living water." But this He spoke of the Spirit, whom those who believed in Him were to receive; for the Spirit was not yet given, because Jesus was not yet glorified.

—JOHN 7:38–39

Justifying the Means

I choose to believe what God says about Himself: that He is good and can be trusted. I recognize that God is not the abuser; rather, people who misuse their authority are the abusers.

Read: Much of the conflict and abuse in churches and ministries comes from the mistaken belief that worthwhile goals justify the means necessary to achieve them. This simply isn't true, and nothing like this is taught in the New Testament. This doesn't seem to matter to many religious leaders, however. They erroneously believe that as long as their goals are good and achievable, their methods are justifiable.

Consequently, if you—or anyone else—gets in their way, you're "out of God's will" and impeding His work. They really believe this, and it's where much of the abuse in Christianity originates. Because of this spurious belief, many church leaders don't scrutinize their methods adequately, and emotional carnage ensues.

In the rubble of this carnage, people who are abused begin to connect their abusers with God, and the line between the two becomes quickly blurred.

In nearly every recovery program, one hears an expression like this: *There's no right way to do a wrong thing.* In other words, when someone pursues goals with flawed motives or methods, the results will be equally flawed—regardless of how noble they appear. The ends do not justify the means and never will—not in God's kingdom anyway. When a church leader recognizes this, he always takes care of his *flock* along the way. When he doesn't, the *sheep* suffer the consequences.

If someone claims, "I know God," but doesn't obey God's commandments, that person is a liar and is not living in the truth. (1 JOHN 2:4 NLT)

Pray: Lord, I ask for three things:

- First, give me the wisdom I need to discern the difference between my self-serving abuser and my loving God.
- Second, heal me from the abuse that "flawed thinking" has done to me, and help me to know that my abuser's rationalized actions do not line up with Your purposes and love for me.
- Third, give me a heart to forgive those who have been abusive.

Write: Ask God to show you if there are ways you are trying to "do the right thing the wrong way"—a tactic you may have unwittingly learned from your abuser. Be honest with yourself and with Him. If you discover you are, what can you practically do to correct your course? Make a list of those who have been adversely impacted by your actions, and be willing to make restitution to them.

Reflect

Sitting down, He called the twelve and said to them, "If anyone wants to be first, he shall be last of all and servant of all."

—MARK 9:35

You ask and do not receive, because you ask with wrong motives, so that you may spend it on your pleasures.

—JAMES 4:3

WEEK 6

STEP 5

I recognize that the only way back to a productive
life is exactly the way I came. Therefore,
I commit to repairing my relationship with God
and making amends with everyone I have
wronged along the way.

Introduction

I recognize that the only way back to a productive life is exactly the way I came. Therefore, I commit to repairing my relationship with God and making amends with everyone I have wronged along the way.

If you're trying to reach a specific destination, turning into a dead-end along the way is never a good idea. The farther down the road you travel, the farther back you have to come. It's a road that leads nowhere—probably like the life you've been living since your abusive experience. At first, it may appear to be the right direction, but at some point, you realize it isn't. Turning around and coming back is a good analogy for what you will be doing in step 5.

In this step, you will be addressing two areas. The first is your relationship with God, which we've touched on before but which requires a more concentrated look. This is your vertical relationship and is the easy part, because God is eager to forgive. It doesn't matter how far you've strayed or how wretched your life has become; He's there for you whenever you are willing to acknowledge the error of your ways. He wants you back—no ifs, ands, or buts.

The way back is clear, but you have to be honest with Him, acknowledging the exact nature of your wrongdoing. You can't hedge on this. You must be forthright: "If we confess our sins, He is faithful and righteous to forgive us our sins and to cleanse us from all unrighteousness" (1 John 1:9).

Once you've confessed your wrongdoing and asked for forgiveness, it's over. You're forgiven. You can count on it. You're square with God, and you don't have to worry about the waywardness of your self-defeating behavior ever again. That part is complete, and you can move forward with total confidence that you're clean—that you've been restored. Best of all, God will never hold it against you. With Him, it's as if it never happened.

The second part, which concerns your horizontal relationships, is more difficult. Undoubtedly, your acting-out behavior has impacted others adversely—perhaps quite a few others. You have to address how you've violated each of these people. The list may be long, but it's imperative to make a good faith effort to apologize to each person you've offended. This can be very difficult. Humility doesn't come easily for any of us, but when you address your wrongdoing, you'll find peace about your past behavior. The experience can be very rewarding—regardless of how the offended person responds.

Apologizing for poor behavior is important, but it means very little unless it's accompanied by your willingness to make appropriate amends. This means you change your behavior, repay a debt, or restore whatever else has damaged your relationship with the other person.

You can't overlook step 5. The quality of your recovery depends on it. With this in mind, prepare yourself for the week ahead.

No Place to Go but Up

I recognize that the only way back to a productive life is exactly the way I came. Therefore, I commit to repairing my relationship with God and making amends with everyone I have wronged along the way.

Read: There is nothing easy about being emotionally crushed, especially when it comes at the hands of religious leaders you once trusted completely. In some ways, it's even more difficult than divorce. That's because marital alienation comes from a broken "human" relationship, not from a broken "divine" relationship.

When you became persona non grata at your church or ministry, did the quality of your relationship with God also come into question? Did someone say you had a problem with God, or was it just implied? Whenever this happens, even a subtle innuendo can be devastating, producing guilt, shame, and a crushing sense of unworthiness.

Maybe your estrangement came as a result of a moral failure, and you were treated as an outcast by those who should have offered guidance. Perhaps you've punished yourself ever since because of your behavior and are buried in shame because of what you've done. That's the trouble with immorality. It leaves you with a wicked "hangover."

Since your rejection by Christians, perhaps you've fallen into alcoholism or another addiction. Maybe you've tried to abandon your relationship with God altogether. Many do, but if your relationship with God is dysfunctional, how can you be okay with yourself or with others?

Even if you feel that your initial estrangement from God resulted from the abuse of others, it's your responsibility to turn things around and repair that relationship now. Blaming others only pulls you further away from God and delays your recovery.

To circumvent this cycle, some try to swap God for other belief systems—beliefs that justify deviant behavior, calling them right. But deep inside, you know wrong is wrong—no matter how adamantly you try to rationalize it. You just can't get around it. That is why restoring your relationship with God has to occur before substantial recovery can be achieved.

Here's the question only you can answer: Are you okay with God or not? If not, you know you need to make it right. You have to acknowledge your wrongdoing. You must confess your sins.

Why not swallow your pride and do it? Why not do it today—right now? Nothing in your life will be right until you do.

If we confess our sins, He is faithful and righteous to forgive us our sins and to cleanse us from all unrighteousness. (1 JOHN 1:9)

Pray: Lord, I know I need to return to You, but it's difficult to know where to begin. Please guide me. I need Your help, and more important, I need Your forgiveness. I want to be okay with You. Help me and forgive me, please.

Write: Acknowledge where you are with God right now and ask Him what a repaired relationship would look like. The only way out of where you are is to reconnect with Him. Acknowledge this truth. Then take as long as you need to confess your wrongdoings. Be specific and be thorough, as you list them in your journal or notebook. When you're finished, allow the burden of your guilt to be lifted from you.

Reflect
Have mercy on me, O God,
* because of your unfailing love.*
Because of your great compassion,
* blot out the stain of my sins.*
Wash me clean from my guilt.
* Purify me from my sin.*
For I recognize my rebellion;
* it haunts me day and night.*

—PSALM 51:1–3 NLT

Draw near to God and He will draw near to you. Cleanse your hands, you sinners; and purify your hearts, you double-minded. Be miserable and mourn and weep; let your laughter be turned into mourning, and your joy to gloom. Humble yourselves in the presence of the Lord, and He will exalt you.

—JAMES 4:8–10

When Praying Was Easy

I recognize that the only way back to a productive life is exactly the way I came. Therefore, I commit to repairing my relationship with God and making amends with everyone I have wronged along the way.

Read: Do you remember when your relationship with the Lord was fresh—when prayer was free and easy? It was like talking to your best friend. Everything was safe and spontaneous. If you think about it, can you remember when prayer was rich and rewarding?

After your religious abuse, it wasn't the same, was it? Did praying become more difficult? Perhaps you stopped praying altogether. Because they feel ashamed or angry, many abused people do. That's how destructive religious abuse can be.

Has this been your experience? Did you assume everything was your fault? You may have even believed you were too unworthy to pray.

If this has been your experience, here's some good news for you. You have a right to address your heavenly Father and talk to Him whenever you please. Nobody, regardless of religious credentials, has the ability to impede your prayer life—that is, *unless you allow it.* Once you have a relationship with God, nobody can ever take that from you—regardless of what he or she says or implies.

You don't have to allow this to happen; but if you already have, you can change the dynamics. Let me say it more strongly: You must not allow this to stand. You must guard your birthright—no matter what. It's not just a privilege to be a child of God; it's a right—your right. Cling to it as your most cherished possession, and never allow anyone to interfere with it again.

For you have not received a spirit of slavery leading to fear again, but you have received a spirit of adoption as sons by which we cry out, "Abba! Father!" (ROMANS 8:15)

Pray: Father, somewhere along the way, I've stopped talking to You like I once did. Please forgive me and allow communication between us to flow freely again. Give me insight, so I will never allow another to interfere with our relationship again.

Write: Take time alone with God. Even if you don't know what to say, just be quiet and alone with Him. Be still and know that He is God. During this quiet moment, write Him a letter, asking Him to draw you back into a closer relationship with Him.

Reflect

By this the love of God was manifested in us, that God has sent His only begotten Son into the world so that we might live through Him. In this is love, not that we loved God, but that He loved us and sent His Son to be the propitiation for our sins.

—I JOHN 4:9–10

Losing Your Sense of Belonging

I recognize that the only way back to a productive life is exactly the way I came. Therefore, I commit to repairing my relationship with God and making amends with everyone I have wronged along the way.

Read: When you go through a destructive experience like religious abuse, you lose your sense of belonging. Within a short time, a feeling of being adrift also seems to typify most abused people. Many lose their bearings, making them more susceptible to self-defeating behavior. Although this is human and easy to understand, you don't have to allow this to be your experience.

Here's why. When Christ comes into your life, He never leaves you—not under any circumstances. In spite of the painful episode you've experienced, you are still a child of God and a permanent citizen in His kingdom. You belong—period—and no one can take that away from you. Abusers can mess with your experience, but they can't extricate Christ from your life. They don't have that power—regardless of what they tell you.

If you repeat this to yourself, you can avoid much of the trauma associated with your painful experience. It will still hurt—no doubt about it—but you don't have to continue pursuing a destructive lifestyle. Don't allow it to become a self-fulfilling prophecy. You can minimize the negativity. It's hard, but it can be done.

Remember, no matter how far down you have gone, you have to come back the same way. With that being the case, doesn't it make sense to stop the downward slide sooner than later?

The choice is yours. You will experience some pain during your recovery, but you can keep it to a minimum. In recovery, this is referred to as a "high bottom" rather than a "low bottom."

113

I am convinced that neither death, nor life, nor angels, nor principalities, nor things present, nor things to come, nor powers, nor height, nor depth, nor any other created thing, shall be able to separate us from the love of God, which is in Christ Jesus our Lord. (ROMANS 8:38–39)

Pray: Father, I have felt so lost and confused. Help me stop my self-defeating behavior. Give me clarity and guidance as I begin my journey back.

Write: Spend time reflecting about where you belong. Remind yourself that you are a child of the King—based on your relationship with Christ. Return to what is true. Write a paragraph or two about how you will never allow anyone to come between God and you again.

Reflect

He came to His own, and those who were His own did not receive Him. But as many as received Him, to them He gave the right to become children of God, even to those who believe in His name, who were born, not of blood nor of the will of the flesh nor of the will of man, but of God.

—JOHN 1:11–13

See how great a love the Father has bestowed on us, that we would be called children of God; and such we are. For this reason the world does not know us, because it did not know Him.

—1 JOHN 3:1

Seeing God's Hand

I recognize that the only way back to a productive life is exactly the way I came. I therefore commit to repairing my relationship with God and making amends with everyone I have wronged along the way.

Read: You've probably heard this saying before: "The pure in heart will see God." But what does it mean? Is it just a sweet, idealistic thought, or does it have value for everyday life?

Here's a hint: Christ never said anything that didn't have real, substantive value. Every word out of His mouth had purpose, and understanding this beatitude is essential to your recovery.

When you experience abuse, you become angry, cynical, bitter, and jaded. It's natural and understandable. At the same time, it's like taking a stick and stirring the sandy bottom of a clear stream. Stirring the sand makes the water muddy, and you can no longer see what's happening beneath the surface. The same is true in life.

If you allow poor behavior or toxic emotions to rule you, you'll have substantial trouble understanding God's direction. Everything will seem confused—and for good reason: it is.

If you don't understand what God wants from you, allow Him to purify your heart. Forgive the person who has offended you. Put away the self-defeating behavior of hard-heartedness that has you enslaved by thanking Jesus for forgiving you. Begin to allow Him to purify your heart, and you will understand what God wants from you. You will begin to see God's hand in practically everything.

Some mistakenly believe God will speak to them regardless of their behavior. That simply isn't true, and it's not taught in the New Testament. He loves you, regardless of what you have done, but only the pure in heart have eyes to see God's purposes. It's not a subtle difference, but an entirely different thing. When you learn the distinction, it will be a major step in your recovery. We live in a generation that doesn't value purity, but as a child of God, you have the option to remain pure.

> *Brethren, whatever is true, whatever is honorable, whatever is right, whatever is pure, whatever is lovely, whatever is of good repute, if there is any excellence and if anything worthy of praise, dwell on these things. The things you have learned and received and heard and seen in me, practice these things, and the God of peace will be with you.*
> (PHILIPPIANS 4:8–9)

Pray: Lord, I want to see clearly again. Draw me to You and purify me. Show me what impedes my purity, and give me the courage to make the necessary changes. My only hope is for You to renew Your work in me. This is what I want.

Write: Spend time today alone with God. Dwell on who He is and what He is like, journaling about what you discover. Unless you make a conscious effort to dwell on Him, the default of your heart will take over and you'll stay mired in mediocrity. You need more than a change of behavior. You need a change of heart, and that can come only as God's Spirit works within you.

Reflect
> *Who may ascend into the hill of the LORD?*
> *And who may stand in His holy place?*
> *He who has clean hands and a pure heart,*
> *Who has not lifted up his soul to falsehood*
> *And has not sworn deceitfully.*
> *He shall receive a blessing from the LORD*
> *And righteousness from the God of his salvation.*
> —PSALM 24:3–5

> *Beloved, now we are children of God, and it has not appeared as yet what we will be. We know that when He appears, we will be like Him, because we will see Him just as He is. And everyone who has this hope fixed on Him purifies himself, just as He is pure.*
> —I JOHN 3:2–3

Becoming Reconciliatory

I recognize that the only way back to a productive life is exactly the way I came. Therefore, I commit to repairing my relationship with God and making amends with everyone I have wronged along the way.

Read: Part of repairing your relationship with God is repairing your relationships with those you have offended. This is where the rubber meets the road in recovery—where it gets really tough. It's easy to repair your relationship with God. He's always there and quick to forgive. It's His nature.

It's entirely different with those you have offended along the way—many of whom are less than forgiving. Some may want nothing to do with you and your so called apology, which falls on deaf ears. They may even treat your attempt at reconciliation with contempt and derision. If this happens, it will make it very difficult, but you have to make an effort—regardless of the consequences.

Remember, you are only responsible for *your part* of the problem, not theirs. Since you can't control the outcome, forcing them to reconcile, you aren't responsible for the result either. How others react to your attempt at reconciliation is their responsibility, not yours. Once you've addressed the issue, leave the outcome to God and trust that He will work in the heart of the other person to produce reconciliation in the future.

It takes a tremendous amount of courage to acknowledge you regret past behavior—especially to a spouse, parent, or child—but it must be done. Besides, not owning up to poor behavior will nag at you, never allowing you to rest until you've done it.

When it's over and you've addressed the problem, it's an entirely different story. The relief you experience is palpable. A tremendous weight will be lifted from your shoulders, and your relief will make you feel lighter—

literally. It will be as if a ball and chain have been removed from your life, which makes confrontations worthwhile.

Dear children, let's not merely say that we love each other; let us show the truth by our actions. (1 JOHN 3:18 NLT)

Pray: Lord, give me the courage to go to those I have wronged in the past. Prepare a path for me to follow, and help me follow that path without deviation. Let those I've offended see my remorse, accept my amends, and forgive me.

Write: Take time to list those you have wronged along the way. Be thorough and make amends to everyone on the list—except to those to whom it would cause more harm than good.

Ask God to prepare you and those on your list for the reconciliation that needs to take place. Keep this list, and cross off names as you make amends. It will take time to accomplish this—perhaps a long time, but each person must be contacted—regardless of how long the process requires.

Reflect
If you are presenting your offering at the altar, and there remember that your brother has something against you, leave your offering there before the altar and go; first be reconciled to your brother, and then come and present your offering.
                                        —MATTHEW 5:23–24

Making Restitution

I recognize that the only way back to a productive life is exactly the way I came. Therefore, I commit to repairing my relationship with God and making amends with everyone I have wronged along the way.

Read: After making a heartfelt apology for poor behavior, there's an overwhelming sense of relief, which leaves you gratified and produces a tremendous sense of relief. You say to yourself, "That wasn't nearly as difficult as I thought it was going to be."

If that were all there is to it, you would be correct, but there's another aspect, which is substantially more difficult. It's making amends for what you've done in the past. For example, if someone treated you unkindly and you've maligned that person's character in response, essentially bearing false witness, an appropriate amend would be to go back to those you've deceived and set the record straight. Repaying a debt is another appropriate amends. When the time comes, knowing what to do to achieve reconciliation will not be difficult.

Making amends is necessary despite what has been done to you. Remember, you're the one in recovery. You are responsible for your part, regardless of what the other person may have done to you.

Resolving such a situation is never an easy task. Receiving forgiveness from someone by making an apology is comparatively easy to making amends that are appropriate for the situation. Additionally, making amends runs counter to our prevailing American culture. We want to ask forgiveness while skipping restitution. By believing an apology is all that's required, you might think you're avoiding the most difficult part, but you're also relinquishing your right to a significant blessing.

The restitution process is where profound change in your character can occur. For complete characterlogical change, you have to travel the full distance and make amends for past behavior—for how you yourself have been abusive in your reaction to being abused. In essence, you're saying, "I used to be like this but no longer. As a part of my apology, I make a commitment to never behave like that again. To prove my sincerity, I'm also going back to the people I've decieved, and I'm going to tell them the truth. I'm going to set the record straight. I'm sorry. It will never happen again."

Then do it.

Making amends is difficult—no question about it—but it's the part of recovery that changes you in permanent ways. By doing this, you refuse to circumvent the truth. You refuse to deflect. You refuse to practice denial. You do the tough work that produces permanent change at the core of your being.

You face the truth courageously, knowing that God has your back every step of the way. Responding like this will change you from the inside out. It's where recovery principles weave themselves into the fabric of your being, and character qualities—like honesty and straightforwardness—become a part of you. It's where you become a better person.

Treat others the same way you want them to treat you. (LUKE 6:31)

Pray: Father, I can't possibly engage in making amends unless You give me Your strength and courage to do so. Please help me. Change me in ways that are permanent—in ways others will notice.

Write: Take your list from the previous day, and start taking action by making a call, sending a letter, or sending an email. Do it one at a time, and take as long as you need—just as long as you're not stalling. Be certain to keep your eyes on the Lord every step of the way. Let Him be your strength, especially when the going gets tough, which it will.

Reflect

"Don't sin by letting anger control you." Don't let the sun go down while you are still angry, for anger gives a foothold to the devil.

If you are a thief, quit stealing. Instead, use your hands for good hard work, and then give generously to others in need. Don't use foul or abusive language. Let everything you say be good and helpful, so that your words will be an encouragement to those who hear them.

And do not bring sorrow to God's Holy Spirit by the way you live. Remember, he has identified you as his own, guaranteeing that you will be saved on the day of redemption.

—EPHESIANS 4:26–30 NLT

WEEK 7

STEP 6

I refuse to become like those who have abused me, and I abandon my desire to spread malice because of my pain and anger.

Introduction

*I refuse to become like those who have abused me, and I abandon my
desire to spread malice because of my pain and anger.*

Step 6 is where your commitment to recovery is tested, and it's a place
where it's easy to get stuck. In the aftermath of abuse, being angry is understandable. For a short period, it's even normal and healthy.

The problem is that more people than not become trapped by their
anger, which leads to bitterness, resentment, and irreconcilability. Unfortunately, they don't progress through it. That's not healthy. It leads to a
wasted life—a life God never intended for them to live—and it's certainly
not a life you want for yourself.

Think of it this way: making the effort to turn away from your pride
and your desire for self-vindication can be as difficult as jogging up a hill.
When you jog uphill, you move against gravity, which requires a con-
certed effort to progress forward. It's much more difficult than running
downhill, which requires little effort. By going uphill, however, several
positive things happen. You become stronger, and as you take each step
upward, you gain confidence. You also know you're accomplishing something worthwhile—something that makes you more fit for the inevitable
challenges of life.

It's the same in recovery. It takes real work to abandon your pride, but
that's what you must do. You must make a vigorous effort to stop indulg-
ing in self-pity. You must begin the process of thinking about someone
other than yourself. Doing this is like jogging up a hill. At first, it requires
substantial effort, but it becomes easier the more frequently you do it.

Also, the sooner you stop insisting upon vindication, the sooner the
healing process can begin. If you steadfastly maintain your position, you
will remain stuck. It's impossible to move forward to a peaceful life while
throwing stones. There's no way to flourish while you languish in a rut.

124

You have to let it go—all of it. Nurturing your anger and resentment is like nursing an infection, which keeps you perpetually weakened. You have to take your medicine, which in this case is like draining the infection of all malice, bitterness, and vengeful thoughts. When you do, you'll begin to recover. You'll begin to have a healthier outlook on life.

This is difficult for many people—perhaps most. But although recovery is hard work, it's also rewarding. It helps build character. Because this can be so difficult, step 6 may take more time for you. If it does, that's okay. Take as much time as required, remembering that the goal is your recovery—your complete recovery.

You want to be everything you're capable of being in life, and this can be done only by purging yourself of toxic emotions. Once this happens, you will begin to experience love, joy, peace, patience, and kindness, which is the life you've always wanted for yourself.

Walking Moment by Moment

*I refuse to become like those who have abused me, and I abandon my
desire to spread malice because of my pain and anger.*

Read: Have you ever asked yourself why there are so many abusive church
people? As many as 30 million people have left the churches of their youth.
One of the reasons for this is that many people believe the church to be an
unsafe place for them emotionally.

Back to our question: why are so many people in the church abusive?
I believe the answer, in part, is that numerous church leaders stop walking in the Light. They think they are in the Light, but they are not. Having once had a transforming experience, they enshrine it. They believe
their experience entitles them to have a sense of superiority. They also
exalt their education and their knowledge to validate their actions, which
are frequently insensitive and abrasive. Because of their "profound experience," anything they do is okay in their eyes. After all, they've "been
chosen" to lead.

Those who have fallen prey to religious abuse are often tempted to
heap their pain and anger on others. Understanding more about why your
abuser hurt you may help you not to follow suit, essentially doing the same
thing. Those who hurt you forget that their walk is supposed to be moment by moment, with the Lord providing illumination for the next step
forward and nothing else. They forget they need grace and mercy—just
like everyone else. Because they believe they are superior, they treat others
as less important. They believe that those chosen to lead have a higher calling than those called to follow.

They have lost their compassion, and when someone gets in their way,
they have no problem crushing that person's spirit. In fact, they believe
it is their right and duty to do so—self-absorbed as they have become.
Because they have sanctified their experience, it eventually becomes staid

and puffed up rather than alive and vibrant. Sadly, they flaunt their authority—while assuring people that they remain humble servants of God.

Since we are living by the Spirit, let us follow the Spirit's leading in every part of our lives. (GALATIANS 5:25 NLT)

Pray: Lord, teach me how to follow You moment by moment. Show me how to walk in the light, and keep me from justifying darkness. Instead, teach me to avoid it. Lead me by Your hand.

Write: Think about how to keep your relationship with the Lord fresh rather than stagnant. Spend time this week with activities that contribute to active communication with God. Make a list of the activities that work well for you.

Reflect

Don't participate in the things these people do. For once you were full of darkness, but now you have light from the Lord. So live as people of light! For this light within you produces only what is good and right and true.

Carefully determine what pleases the Lord.

—EPHESIANS 5:7–10 NLT

Trust in the LORD with all your heart
    And do not lean on your own understanding.
In all your ways acknowledge Him,
    And He will make your paths straight.
Do not be wise in your own eyes;
    Fear the LORD and turn away from evil.
It will be healing to your body
    And refreshment to your bones.

—PROVERBS 3:5–8

Becoming Who You Really Are

I refuse to become like those who have abused me, and I abandon my desire to spread malice because of my pain and anger.

Read: When I first experienced religious abuse, I was hurt, angry, and confused. My life became purposeless for a long time. When I realized that wallowing in self-pity wasn't improving my situation, I knew I needed to make some changes. I would never become the person God wanted me to be by nurturing bitterness, and nobody was going to help me. I had to help myself.

That's when I made the determination not to spread malice to others because of my pain. That's also when I stopped my downward slide and started working to recover what I had lost. Realizing God was not the problem, but the solution, I looked to Him and the words He spoke as my source of courage and inspiration. I looked to God for hope—for a way out of my emotional pit. I had to rethink nearly every aspect of my life, changing practically everything. At first, I was overwhelmed by the daunting task before me, resenting all that needed to be done. After a while, knowing my attitude was self-defeating, I chose to embrace the work ahead of me instead.

When I was much younger, I had a vision for what my life would be—a vision that was quite grandiose—but God's purpose was different. Becoming who He wanted me to be has taken substantial effort, and it continues to take regular work. By looking to God for the future rather than blaming Him for the past, I chose life over the debilitating half-life of bitterness.

I worked out a new purpose—a more realistic one. Now that I've lived it for many years, I can't imagine I was created for anything else. Although I have setbacks, my life is filled with the peace and contentment I always desired but was never able to achieve.

Work hard to show the results of your salvation, obeying God with deep reverence and fear. (PHILIPPIANS 2:12 NLT)

Pray: Lord, enable me to see You as the solution to my problems and not the cause of them. Help me to uncomplicate my life as I focus my eyes on Your will for me, not my will for me.

Write: Take some time to journal what your role is in your recovery. You must play your part, but you must also be clear about what that is. Be as specific as you know how to be. Once you've written it, ask God for the courage and strength to accomplish it.

Reflect

By grace you have been saved through faith; and that not of yourselves, it is the gift of God; not as a result of works, so that no one may boast.
—EPHESIANS 2:8–9

Once we, too, were foolish and disobedient. We were misled and became slaves to many lusts and pleasures. Our lives were full of evil and envy, and we hated each other.

But—"When God our Savior revealed his kindness and love, he saved us, not because of the righteous things we had done, but because of his mercy. He washed away our sins, giving us a new birth and new life through the Holy Spirit. He generously poured out the Spirit upon us through Jesus Christ our Savior."
—TITUS 3:3–6 NLT

Pride Rears Its Ugly Head

I refuse to become like those who have abused me, and I abandon my desire to spread malice because of my pain and anger.

Read: Very few religious leaders begin their sojourn with the express purpose of being spiritually abusive. Like everyone else who is committed to God, they start out being humble. Recognizing their sinfulness, they ask for and accept God's grace and mercy.

Something happens to many of them along the way, however. After walking the walk for a while—perhaps a long while—they become good at superficial conformity to a wholesome lifestyle. They develop a measure of self-control, becoming smug and self-satisfied. At some level, they forget it was the mercy of God that brought them to Him in the first place. Because they don't have any glaring, outward manifestations of self-defeating behavior, they start to believe they are better than those who do. From their perspective, this makes them superior to those around them.

When this occurs, pride rears its ugly head, which frequently leads to spiritual abuse. All that is needed is for something to happen that falls outside of the guidelines of their carefully constructed, self-righteous belief system. When it does, all hell breaks loose—literally. In their zeal, they have no idea that what they are doing is harmful, destructive, and wrong. In fact, they are certain their actions are warranted. They genuinely believe their abusiveness is doing God's will. That's how deceptive self-righteousness can become.

When you look at it from this perspective, abusive people are quite pitiful. Take a minute and think about your situation. Can you see where the self-righteousness of your abuser was operational? Perhaps you've also had a problem with being self-righteous at one time or another. Most people have, especially Christians.

What sorrow awaits you teachers of religious law and you Pharisees. Hypocrites! For you are like whitewashed tombs—beautiful on the outside but filled on the inside with dead people's bones and all sorts of impurity. Outwardly you look like righteous people, but inwardly your hearts are filled with hypocrisy and lawlessness. (MATTHEW 23:27–28 NLT)

Pray: Lord, help me understand those who have been abusive to me. Help me see the wrong for what it is, and help me to develop a forgiving spirit toward them. Please guard me from the same behavior.

Write: Now take a giant step in your recovery, and pray for those who abused you. Write your prayer out, and be specific. Regardless of how unpleasant it is, make the effort. If it's difficult, persevere. It will begin the process of breaking the chains of your emotional imprisonment.

Reflect

Two men went to the Temple to pray. One was a Pharisee, and the other was a despised tax collector. The Pharisee stood by himself and prayed this prayer: "I thank you, God, that I am not a sinner like everyone else. For I don't cheat, I don't sin, and I don't commit adultery. I'm certainly not like that tax collector! I fast twice a week, and I give you a tenth of my income."

But the tax collector stood at a distance and dared not even lift his eyes to heaven as he prayed. Instead, he beat his chest in sorrow, saying, "O God, be merciful to me, for I am a sinner." I tell you, this sinner, not the Pharisee, returned home justified before God. For those who exalt themselves will be humbled, and those who humble themselves will be exalted.

—LUKE 18:10–14 NLT

The Spirit of Self-Vindication

*I refuse to become like those who have abused me, and I abandon my
desire to spread malice because of my pain and anger.*

Read: When you've been abused by someone in a position of authority,
you experience many thoughts and emotions. One is the spirit of self-
vindication. Because you've been wronged, there is a desire to retaliate. It
can even become a compulsion. You want to "set the record straight."

You say to yourself—or to anyone who will listen—"I'm not going to
let him get away with this. I'm going to . . ." Then you proceed to explain
how you are going to even the score, even if it's just by talking to yourself
about it.

This is where things get tricky. You may be right about your abuser's
need to be stopped, but if your motive is wrong, then you are in danger of
becoming exactly like the one who abused you. That's when the spirit of
self-vindication produces another layer of self-righteousness. You become
like your abuser.

When you act on this vindictive spirit, you are taking matters into your
own hands. You try to force an outcome, and that rarely works. It feels
great at first, but the satisfaction is short lived. The fruit from it is bitter,
and you are either forced to make amends or justify your poor behavior
from then on—exactly like the person who abused you.

Only the very brave have the courage to apologize and make amends.
Most choose to rationalize their retaliation as just—even if it's a harsh
word spoken spitefully—reaping a hard heart in the process. Being vengeful only works in movies and cartoons. In real life, it's rarely a worthwhile
option.

*Do not go on passing judgment before the time, but wait until the
Lord comes who will both bring to light the things hidden in the*

darkness and disclose the motives of men's hearts; and then each man's praise will come to him from God. (1 CORINTHIANS 4:5)

Pray: Father, if I have a spirit of hatred, help me see it clearly. This isn't what I want. I want to have a reconcilable spirit. Please guard me from a hard heart and a hateful, vengeful spirit.

Write: Write out the vengeful thoughts you've had toward your abuser. After you've done this, spend time considering your heart before God. What do you see? Are you walking in humility and forgiveness, or are you nurturing a vengeful spirit?

Reflect

Do not be deceived, God is not mocked; for whatever a man sows, this he will also reap. For the one who sows to his own flesh will from the flesh reap corruption, but the one who sows to the Spirit will from the Spirit reap eternal life. Let us not lose heart in doing good, for in due time we will reap if we do not grow weary.

—GALATIANS 6:7–9

He who does wrong will receive the consequences of the wrong which he has done, and that without partiality.

—COLOSSIANS 3:25

An Abusive Mind-set

I refuse to become like those who have abused me, and I abandon my desire to spread malice because of my pain and anger.

Read: When people are spiritually abused, an interesting phenomenon often develops. They take on a mind-set exactly like their abusers'. The abusee also becomes self-righteous, lashing out at their perpetrators in the same cruel, venomous way.

Each abused person, however, believes his wrath is justified because of his earlier experience at the hands of his abuser. He rarely puts it together that it's the same thing. Although he may make a distinction, there is no difference—none whatsoever.

Abusive behavior is abusive behavior, regardless of who initiates it. That's the nature of self-righteousness. It's an attitude that justifies itself. That's why it's called *self*-righteousness.

I understand the pain and humiliation of your experience, but guess what? If you continue insisting you are right and "he is wrong," you will never heal. You're stuck, and you'll stay stuck—just like a car in a mud hole. Although the tire spins faster and faster as you press down on the accelerator in a vain effort to extricate yourself, there is never any progress. It spins aimlessly but dangerously. Because of your anger, you become emotionally isolated as your friends back away from you, figuratively and literally.

Is that what you want for your life? Do you want to nurture bitterness, wasting years that become decades? Do you want the people you love to withdraw from you, weary of your negativity?

Of course, you don't. But that's what will happen unless you acknowledge the pride and anger in your heart. You have to make a conscious, determined effort to turn away from it. You have to let go, all of it.

Peter came to him and asked, "Lord, how often should I forgive someone who sins against me? Seven times?"

"No, not seven times," Jesus replied, "but seventy times seven!"
(MATTHEW 18:21–22 NLT)

Pray: Lord, help me see the state of my heart honestly and clearly. Show me the pride and anger inside me. Guide me in how to deal with what I find. Help me to let go of all my negativity, which poisons my soul and spreads malice. Then help me develop a spirit of reconciliation.

Write: Pride and anger are deadly sins. Pride is considered the granddaddy of all sins. It began in the garden of Eden. As you look at your areas of self-defeating behavior, consider how each can be traced back to the root of pride. Name and write down at least one instance when your pride and anger have adversely affected you. Next, ask God to cleanse and change you in these areas. He is your hope to attain the fruitful life you desire.

Reflect

When you follow the desires of your sinful nature, the results are very clear: sexual immorality, impurity, lustful pleasures, idolatry, sorcery, hostility, quarreling, jealousy, outbursts of anger, selfish ambition, dissension, division, envy, drunkenness, wild parties, and other sins like these. Let me tell you again, as I have before, that anyone living that sort of life will not inherit the Kingdom of God.

But the Holy Spirit produces this kind of fruit in our lives: love, joy, peace, patience, kindness, goodness, faithfulness, gentleness, and self-control. There is no law against these things!

Those who belong to Christ Jesus have nailed the passions and desires of their sinful nature to his cross and crucified them there. Since we are living by the Spirit, let us follow the Spirit's leading in every part of our lives. Let us not become conceited, or provoke one another, or be jealous of one another.

—GALATIANS 5:19–26 NLT

Self-Vindication Doesn't Work

I refuse to become like those who have abused me, and I abandon my desire to spread malice because of my pain and anger.

Read: When you've been abused, when you've been verbally maligned, when you've had your character assaulted by someone you trusted, the most natural thing in the world to do is strike back. You want to retaliate. You want to vindicate yourself. You want to set the record straight so that everybody will know the truth. You want someone to listen.

For those of us in recovery from religious abuse, we know these feelings well. It's nearly impossible for us to escape them—especially when the incident is fresh.

Unfortunately, the abusive leaders are in the position of power. Any attempt to set the record straight routinely falls on deaf ears, making the abusee seem like a disgruntled malcontent.

Although it's difficult to survive abusiveness, you need to renew your mind by seeking the kingdom of God first, as Jesus said in Matthew 6: "Seek first His kingdom, and His righteousness, and all these things will be added to you" (Matthew 6:33). As you focus on His kingdom, you must allow God to set the record straight—in His time, not yours. To pursue a vengeful spirit will make you an abusive person—exactly like the person who abused you.

From your perspective, this may seem particularly unfair, but if you seek God's perspective diligently, your perspective will change. And your vindication will come. For most of us, instant gratification isn't fast enough. From God's perspective, rebuilding you from the inside out is far more important than proving to the world that you are right.

Never take your own revenge, beloved, but leave room for the wrath of God, for it is written, "Vengeance is mine, I will repay," says the Lord. (ROMANS 12:19)

Pray: Lord, help me develop a good attitude about my abuse. Give me wisdom to understand the lesson instead of insisting that I be understood. Enable me to keep my mind focused on You rather than on being "right."

Write: Take time to consider your motives. Do you insist on being "right"? True forgiveness is relinquishing your right to be vindicated. It says, "What you have done is wrong, but I choose to let go of it—to forgive it." Open the door to greater freedom in your life by seeking to forgive your abuser. Write the name of one person you refuse to forgive on a sheet of paper. Now allow the Lord to forgive your abuser through you with His forgiveness. Finally, tear up the sheet of paper.

Reflect

Humble yourselves before God. Resist the devil, and he will flee from you. Come close to God, and God will come close to you. Wash your hands, you sinners; purify your hearts, for your loyalty is divided between God and the world.

—JAMES 4:7–8 NLT

The LORD also will be a stronghold for the oppressed,
A stronghold in times of trouble;
And those who know Your name will put their trust in You,
For You, O LORD, have not forsaken those who seek You.

—PSALM 9:9–10

STEP 7

I will make a detailed, written account of my abusive experiences as well as my subsequent behavior. I commit to being as thorough and honest as I'm able.

Introduction

I will make a detailed, written account of my abusive experiences as well as my subsequent behavior. I commit to being as thorough and honest as I'm able.

Much of steps 1 through 6 are vertical in nature—pertaining to your relationship with God. Putting your relationship with Him in order is the most important part of recovery. It's the key to freedom. Until you are on solid footing with Him, little progress can be accomplished, and your behavior will not change substantially. At best, you will learn to talk the talk. You may fool others, but your insides will still be hollow and disquieted. To become the vibrant person you were created to be, you must reconnect with God, which requires substantial soul-searching.

Even though this step entails spelling out your personal experience in substantial detail, it's when you begin to turn your attention from yourself toward others.

For many, this part of recovery may be very difficult. Often people prefer to "let sleeping dogs lie," refusing to dredge up the past. They believe this course of inaction is wise, but it isn't. They're just fooling themselves—exalting their rationalizations and ascribing wisdom to them.

If the dogs had been sleeping, there wouldn't be debilitating emotional pain or self-defeating behavior, would there? Since anger, guilt, shame, and many other toxic emotions keep the lives of abused people in perpetual turmoil, the dogs have been anything but sleeping.

You will not recover without taking an accurate inventory, both of what happened to you and how you may have subsequently acted out.

As you prepare for this week, make a commitment to be completely forthright about the abuse you've experienced—as well as your subsequent behavior. Without scrupulous honesty, most of the value of step 7 will be lost. If you are determined to be honest, much of the pain from your past will fade and soon become a distant memory.

In recovery, there is a saying: "You are only as sick as your secrets."

Like so many pithy statements, it's surprisingly accurate. Step 7 is your opportunity to expose your conduct to the light—expose it to God. It can be difficult—no doubt about it. At the same time, it's freeing. Presently, you may have the weight of the world on your shoulders, producing significant apprehension. It may make you want to quit or at least put off step 7 for a while—a long while.

Resist this urge at all costs. Be courageous and move forward. The reward is worth it—guaranteed.

Embracing Your Pain

I will make a detailed, written account of my abusive experiences as well as my subsequent behavior. I commit to being as thorough and honest as I'm able.

Read: Writing about your experience, being as honest as you know how to be, may be quite painful and difficult. It may feel similar to when the incident first occurred. If this happens, it's a good thing and should be welcomed rather than avoided. It's what you want to happen. By embracing your pain and acknowledging your feelings as you write about them, you will decrease their power over you, not increase it. This makes it much easier to release those feelings.

Your pain, which has been debilitating in the past, will begin to diminish. It's like lancing a boil. It's always painful for a moment, but once it's done, the festering infection below the surface will begin to diminish. It's the same when you address your abusive experience head-on. You neutralize its power to produce shame, despair, and other toxic emotions in your heart and in your soul.

That's why step 7 is so important. It's where your recovery begins to take concrete form. It's when you start to feel whole once again. While writing, there may be a tendency to repress some of your experience. If this happens, redouble your efforts to be transparent. If you don't, you will make little progress. Although you may have been guarding your wounds or even nurturing them, that's not what step 7 requires. You need to be fearlessly honest about what happened.

Be courageous in your soul-searching. Regardless of what the truth is, you need to express it—in writing. Because truth sets you free, you need to be absolutely transparent. Nothing less will suffice. If you refuse to lance this painful boil, you'll remain stuck, and you will have to repeat step 7 again and again—until you can be completely honest with yourself.

Jesus said to the people who believed in him, "You are truly my disciples if you remain faithful to my teachings. And you will know the truth, and the truth will set you free." (JOHN 8:31–32 NLT)

Pray: God, give me the courage I need to face my past. Help me be more honest than I've ever been. Help me to be candid with myself and with You. I know that without Your help, I'll never move forward.

Write: Take time today to begin writing about your abuse. It may be painful, but you need to make the effort.

Reflect

Behold, You desire truth in the innermost being,
And in the hidden part You will make me know wisdom.
Purify me with hyssop, and I shall be clean;
Wash me, and I shall be whiter than snow.

—PSALM 51:6–7

If we say that we have no sin, we are deceiving ourselves and the truth is not in us. If we confess our sins, He is faithful and righteous to forgive us our sins and to cleanse us from all unrighteousness.

—I JOHN 1:8–9

Review Your Written Account

I will make a detailed, written account of my abusive experience as well as my subsequent behavior. I commit to being as thorough and honest as I'm able.

Read: By now, you should have made a good start at getting the story of your abuse on paper. Although writing about what happened may be painful, it's a necessary step in your recovery. Now it's time to take a harder, more penetrating look at what you've written. As you review it a second, third, or even a fourth time, you will remember additional things that will make your written account more thorough—more complete.

As you begin to feel relief about the past, you'll want to be more thorough than when you first began the process—the more thorough, the better. The more honest you can be, the easier it is to free yourself from the toxic emotions that have held you captive to the past and to your abuse.

By being thorough and honest, you'll begin to break the chains that have held you captive for so long. In time—maybe even a short time—the sting from your abuse will begin to fade, and you will be free to walk into the future, unencumbered by the past.

It's at this point that true wisdom, God's wisdom, will enter your heart, and you will begin to see everything in life more clearly. When this happens—and it will—the destructive power from your abuse will be broken and will lose its debilitating power over you.

To you who are willing to listen, I say, love your enemies! Do good to those who hate you. Bless those who curse you. Pray for those who hurt you. (LUKE 6:27–28 NLT)

Pray: God, as I write about the truth of my experience, please free me from the toxic emotions that have held me captive for so long. Give me the courage I need to be honest with myself and with You.

Write: Take time to go deeper into your written account of your experiences. Reread what you have written, and take a more penetrating look inside. Remember, you are cleaning house, and the more thorough you clean, the better.

Reflect

The wisdom from above is first pure, then peaceable, gentle, reasonable, full of mercy and good fruits, unwavering, without hypocrisy.

—JAMES 3:17

Give instruction to a wise man and he will be still wiser,
    Teach a righteous man and he will increase his learning.
The fear of the LORD is the beginning of wisdom,
    And the knowledge of the Holy One is understanding.
For by me your days will be multiplied,
    And years of life will be added to you.

—PROVERBS 9:9–11

Admitting Your Wrong Behavior

I will make a detailed, written account of my abusive experiences as well as my subsequent behavior. I commit to being as thorough and honest as I'm able.

Read: As you write the narrative of your abusive experience, you also need to begin writing about your subsequent misbehavior. As stated repeatedly, complete honesty is required—not just about what happened to you but also how you have responded to the abusive situation. For some, it's not difficult to write about being abused. After all, you've likely replayed it repeatedly in your mind since it happened—especially when the incident first occurred.

But being completely candid about your subsequent responsibility may be much more challenging. Here's why. In our minds, we want God to take our side about everything—no questions asked. We want Him to vindicate us completely. We've been victimized, and it's His responsibility to correct the situation. We're right; they're wrong. It's as simple as that. All that's missing is God's rubber stamp on our position.

Unfortunately, there's usually another side to the story—a side we rarely think about. It's how we've responded and its negative impact on others. In step 7, you have to look at *your* behavior and take full responsibility for your actions. As you reread what you've written, ask yourself incisive questions—especially about your behavior. Ask yourself questions like these:

- Have I condemned the actions of others while minimizing my own?
- Have I considered my behavior to be understandable and justifiable, considering the situation?
- Have I given myself a pass about what I've done—a pass I'm unwilling to extend to others?

146

- Have I extended grace and mercy to myself while demanding the letter of the law for my abusers?

Most have a tendency to remember being wronged while disregarding the wrong they themselves have done. We want to give ourselves a pass because we acted out of our pain and disillusionment. As we see it, our poor behavior is understandable—maybe even justifiable. It's not the same for others. We want them held completely accountable.

An abused person's perspective becomes distorted. Remember, you are just as responsible for your behavior as your abuser. That's why so much reflection is required. You need to examine your conduct and the state of your heart. Be fearlessly honest. Remember, the goal of step 7 is to heal, not to excuse or minimize your poor behavior.

Examine me, O LORD, and try me;
Test my mind and my heart. (PSALM 26:2)

Pray: Father, give me the courage to take full responsibility for all of the self-destructive behavior I've engaged in since I experienced my abusive situation. Please, don't allow me to be defensive but to be fearlessly honest. I know I need to take my eyes off of myself and the pain I've suffered. Please help me with this.

Write: Write about your experience—all of it. Also begin to write about your own behavior that resulted from your abuse. Be as forthright as you know how to be, resisting the temptation to skirt over your wrongdoing. When you've finished, you will have made progress in your recovery.

Reflect
I confessed all my sins to you
and stopped trying to hide my guilt.
I said to myself, "I will confess my rebellion to the LORD."
And you forgave me! All my guilt is gone.

Therefore, let all the godly pray to you while there is still time,
that they may not drown in the floodwaters of judgment.
—PSALM 32:5–6 NLT

He who conceals his transgressions will not prosper,
 But he who confesses and forsakes them will find compassion.
How blessed is the man who fears always,
 But he who hardens his heart will fall into calamity.
—PROVERBS 28:13–14

You Are Still Responsible

I will make a detailed, written account of my abusive experiences as well as my subsequent behavior. I commit to being as thorough and honest as I'm able.

Read: Writing about your subsequent behavior—your conduct after being abused—should prove to be very enlightening. As always, be certain to be thorough. It will help.

For many, acting-out behavior is very typical after an abusive episode—excessive drinking, promiscuity, viewing pornography, abusing prescriptions, overeating, or whatever it takes to numb the stinging pain of humiliation and rejection. Because your emotions are out of balance, so is your ability to restrain your behavior. Many abandon moderation and cling to excess. In time, efforts at self-medication may become a problem greater than the original one, as your direction in life becomes cloudier. Your behavior becomes self-defeating in every sense of the word. Eventually, nothing seems to go right, and you sink deeper into despair.

Because the acting-out behavior causes its own set of problems, you need to be as rigorously honest about it as you are about your abuse. It's the only way to untangle your life. It will not work to say your situation was caused by an outside event like abuse. You're still responsible for your actions—all of them. To turn your life around, you need to be completely forthright about the compromises you've made—about behavior you would rather not reveal. The more ashamed you are about your actions, the more you need to write about them. You have to come completely clean.

When you do, a tremendous weight will be lifted from you as you unburden your mind and your soul. You're doing the work necessary to break the chains that have held you captive for so long.

It was for freedom that Christ set us free; therefore keep standing firm and do not be subject again to a yoke of slavery. (GALATIANS 5:1)

Pray: Father, give me the courage to face the truth about my behavior. Thank You for loving and accepting me—no matter what I've done. Thank You for being a forgiving God. Thank You for forgiving me.

Write: Take time to write about your acting-out behavior. Be specific. Don't allow anything to get in the way of taking time to do this critical step.

Reflect

Be gracious to me, O God, according to Your loving kindness;
According to the greatness of Your compassion blot out my
transgressions.
Wash me thoroughly from my iniquity
And cleanse me from my sin.
For I know my transgressions,
And my sin is ever before me.
Against You, You only, I have sinned
And done what is evil in Your sight,
So that You are justified when You speak
And blameless when You judge. . . .

Behold, You desire truth in the innermost being,
And in the hidden part You will make me know wisdom.
Purify me with hyssop, and I shall be clean;
Wash me, and I shall be whiter than snow.
Make me to hear joy and gladness,
Let the bones which You have broken rejoice.
Hide Your face from my sins
And blot out all my iniquities.

Create in me a clean heart, O God,
And renew a steadfast spirit within me.

—PSALM 51:1–4, 6–10

Scrupulous Honesty

I will make a detailed, written account of my abusive experiences as well as my subsequent behavior. I commit to being as thorough and honest as I'm able.

Read: As you get deeper into journaling about your experiences, your state of mind will be your most important asset or your greatest liability, either helping you or hindering you greatly. Obviously, you want it to help rather than hinder.

This is not the time for vindication or heaping blame and condemnation upon others. In fact, the exact opposite is required. To heal, you must abandon your insistence upon retribution. Step 7 is about you and your healing—not about "them." If you insist on making it about how badly you were wronged, you will not make much progress. Justifying your behavior while condemning others will get you nowhere.

You must abandon your anger and your need to be right. Instead of pursuing self-righteous vindication, embrace your woundedness, admit your wrongdoings, and acknowledge precisely who you are. Covering the truth with a blanket of false superiority never works in life, and it certainly will not work in recovery. Make a conscious choice to be the precise opposite. Be candid. Be transparent. Be proactively forthright about your subsequent behavior.

In an effort to be self-protective, many wounded people try to fool themselves and others, constructing elaborate facades that bear little resemblance to the truth. They project a false image and try to convince themselves and others it is true. This facade becomes their reality.

Living a lie isn't taking good care of yourself. If you want to heal, you have to abandon your denial and embrace the truth. You have to be exactly who you say you are—regardless of who that may be.

Stop pretending to be what you are not. Be who you are, and allow

God's healing touch to reach down and pick you up. It doesn't matter how far you've fallen. In fact, the Scriptures teach that the person who has been forgiven much is capable of more love than the one who has been forgiven little. All that's required is scrupulous honesty. With it, all things are possible. Without it, you'll continue to languish—unfulfilled in life.

> *I tell you, her sins—and they are many—have been forgiven, so she has shown me much love. But a person who is forgiven little shows only little love.* (LUKE 7:47 NLT)

Pray: Father, help me with my state of mind. Help me to be honest with myself. Enable me to approach my recovery with humility and honesty—not with self-righteousness and self-protectiveness.

Write: Spend an extra five minutes alone with God today. Take time to calm your fears about peeling away the layers of denial as you write about your own wrongdoing and self-destructive behavior. Soak in who He is and how much He loves you. Don't underestimate your need for admitting where you are right now. It's a valuable recovery tool.

Reflect

> *Blessed be the God and Father of our Lord Jesus Christ, who has blessed us with every spiritual blessing in the heavenly places in Christ, just as He chose us in Him before the foundation of the world, that we would be holy and blameless before Him. In love He predestined us to adoption as sons through Jesus Christ to Himself, according to the kind intention of His will, to the praise of the glory of His grace, which He freely bestowed on us in the Beloved.*
> —EPHESIANS 1:3–6

> *For God so loved the world, that He gave His only begotten Son, that whoever believes in Him shall not perish, but have eternal life.*
> —JOHN 3:16

Making Progress in Your Recovery

I will make a detailed, written account of my abusive experiences as well as my subsequent behavior. I commit to being as thorough and honest as I'm able.

Read: After you've completed writing your inventory, beginning with the more serious issues and then proceeding to the less serious, you will have made huge strides toward recovery—toward healing. The expression "confession is good for the soul" is accurate, and the most important person to tell the truth to is yourself.

By putting everything on paper and reviewing it numerous times, it's hard to maintain an attitude of denial. Even if you begin that way, you'll make appropriate changes as you reread what you've written. That's the way your conscience works, and it's a good thing. Be sensitive to it.

You may want to keep what you've written and refer to it from time to time. Many people do. Some read what they've written every year to measure their progress in recovery. If you decide to do this, you'll be amazed at the progress you've made as the years go by. It can be quite encouraging, or if you regress, it can help you get back on track. It's like a photographic image, capturing who you are at a specific point in time.

This process is so rewarding that you may utilize this exercise routinely to help sort out other difficult issues. People in recovery from substance abuse do this all the time. It becomes a part of them—a part of who they are. By writing about difficult situations, you'll learn how to get a handle on the pain from your abuse and your motives in subsequent behavior. By writing about your feelings, you will gain insights that will help you get back on track when you stumble. This step, though difficult, will serve you well in days to come and ensure a recovery that only honesty can bring.

Remember from where you have fallen, and repent and do the deeds
you did at first; or else I am coming to you and will remove your
lampstand out of its place—unless you repent. (REVELATION 2:5)

Pray: God, enable me to get in touch with my pain and the motives for
my self-destructive behavior. Help me to be honest with myself, and give
me insight about my role in the abuse.

Write: Reread your account of both your abusive experience and your
subsequent misbehavior. Ask God if there is anything missing. Be sure
to include your feelings in this document. Remember, your feelings are
okay—no matter what they are.

Reflect
The plans of the heart belong to man,
  But the answer of the tongue is from the LORD.
All the ways of a man are clean in his own sight,
  But the LORD weighs the motives.
Commit your works to the LORD,
  And your plans will be established.
                          —PROVERBS 16:1–3

You are great and do wondrous deeds;
  You alone are God.
Teach me Your way, O LORD;
  I will walk in Your truth;
  Unite my heart to fear Your name.
I will give thanks to You, O Lord my God, with all my heart,
  And will glorify Your name forever.
                          —PSALM 86:10–12

WEEK 9

STEP 8

I will share my experience and my own wrongdoing with a trusted friend, confessing the exact state of my heart.

Introduction

I will share my experience and my own wrongdoing with a trusted friend, confessing the exact state of my heart.

We live in a society where real intimacy is virtually nonexistent. We have drifted so far from it that few even know what it is. If you ask someone to define it, the definition will more than likely focus on sexual intimacy and little else. The two have become virtually synonymous.

There's much more to intimacy than its sexual aspects, however. Intimacy is being connected to another human being at the deepest level of who you are, which does not require a sexual relationship at all. There's nothing physical about the kind of intimacy required in step 8.

True intimacy allows another human being to understand exactly who you are—warts and all. It invites that person into your life at the deepest level—into your head, into your heart, and into your experiences. It involves allowing another human to know your deepest thoughts, your deepest aspirations. It means being vulnerable by being completely transparent.

When you empower another to share in your heartaches as well as your joys, you trust that person with your soul, with the essence of who you are. You are open and honest—without fear of condemnation—to someone who will accept you exactly the way you are and gently guide you, while providing encouragement.

Nearly everyone wants to be connected with another person at this level, but it's difficult in our world where electronic communication devices such as iPods and BlackBerrys, replace communication with others. In this era, we allow people in—but not very far.

In the twenty-first century, women feel closer to Oprah than to their girlfriends. Men rarely communicate about anything deeper than sports or funny jokes. In our culture, intimacy is rare and becoming rarer.

To achieve the level of recovery you require, old-fashioned intimacy is necessary—both horizontally and vertically. That's why step 8 is so important. It requires you to go outside of yourself to tell another person exactly who you are.

Because alienation from people and from God is now the norm, it's not as easy as it used to be. Nevertheless, it's absolutely necessary. Finding a trustworthy person may intimidate you, but you can do it.

The Linchpin to Recovery

I will share my experience and my own wrongdoing with a trusted friend, confessing the exact state of my heart.

Read: The Scriptures tell us to confess our sins to one another and pray for one another that we may be healed (see James 5:16). There is nothing more important to complete recovery from religious abuse than confession. Remember again this poignant saying from Alcoholics Anonymous: *You are only as sick as your secrets.* It's painfully true. What you hide does keep you emotionally unhealthy.

Once something troubling you has been revealed—exposed to the light—it's like the venom has been removed from a bite, rendering it harmless. The debilitating power of the problem, regardless of the issue, begins to dissipate. The freeing power of God's love is then released to heal and restore you to wholeness.

As long as you hide what's troubling you, you're destined to live in fear—with a soul sickness that works like poison, keeping you from being everything God intends you to be. Hiding the dark places that exist in your soul denies reality and leaves you wounded, unable to see reality clearly.

This is where the rubber meets the road, because step 8 requires you to go outside of yourself. It requires you to trust—totally and unreservedly—another human being. Yet many people are not trustworthy, which means you must exercise caution and discernment before exposing your vulnerability to another.

Confess your sins to one another, and pray for one another so that you may be healed. (JAMES 5:16)

Pray: Father, the idea of talking to someone openly about what is going on inside of me is scary and uncomfortable. Give me the courage to open up and the wisdom to know whom I can trust.

Write: Come up with a list of people you believe could be trusted with the details of what has happened in your life. Ask God whom you should approach to talk to about your abuse. Be aware it is unwise to discuss your wounds with too many people. Guard yourself. Just as talking to no one does not aid your recovery, revealing too much to too many may have the same result. Maintaining a balance in this area is essential.

Reflect
> *He who conceals his transgressions will not prosper,*
> > *But he who confesses and forsakes them will find compassion.*
> *How blessed is the man who fears always,*
> > *But he who hardens his heart will fall into calamity.*
> > > —PROVERBS 28:13–14

Whom to Trust

I will share my experience and my own wrongdoing with a trusted friend, confessing the exact state of my heart.

Read: If confession is good for the soul, then acknowledging your wrongdoing is necessary for healing and maintaining health. Confession is one of the seven sacraments in Roman Catholicism, and the sacredness of the confessional has been institutionalized for centuries.

For non-Catholics, confession is one of the ways religious abuse occurs most frequently. When a person unburdens his or her soul to someone considered trustworthy, often what is revealed is used against the penitent through gossip, condemnation, or loss of standing in the church. It's one of the primary reasons this book is a critical need in Protestant churches and recovery communities.

The way to determine who to trust with the most intimate details of your soul is clear. Don't trust those who have not already proven themselves worthy of your trust. The importance of this cannot be overstated. If you trust someone who is unworthy, your best efforts at transparency will prove to be counterproductive.

Before you open up, ask yourself and the other person some pointed questions about what you want and expect from the confession. If the other person doesn't respond in a loving, understanding, and accepting way, don't proceed. Find someone else.

There are many people who have the maturity, discernment, and discretion necessary to help. Be patient until you find the right person. Someone will emerge or be brought into your life. If not, talk with a professional counselor. In that way, you can be assured of confidentiality.

He who goes about as a talebearer reveals secrets,
But he who is trustworthy conceals a matter. (PROVERBS 11:13)

Pray: Father, thank You that You don't want me to carry my burden alone. Please make it clear to whom I should open up my life. Help me find someone trustworthy.

Write: After thinking about your list from yesterday, which two or three people seem to be the safest to talk to? Write down some pointed questions you can use to "screen" these people. Again, if during your meeting with them, they don't respond in a loving, accepting way, don't proceed. If there is no one on your "safe" list, ask God to bring another person into your life—a safe one.

Reflect
Though good advice lies deep within the heart,
*   a person with understanding will draw it out.*

Many will say they are loyal friends,
*   but who can find one who is truly reliable?*

The godly walk with integrity;
*   blessed are their children who follow them.*
                                    —PROVERBS 20:5–7 NLT

Finding a Safe Person

I will share my experience and my own wrongdoing with a trusted friend, confessing the exact state of my heart.

Read: When selecting someone to trust, be thoughtful about the process, not impulsive. Far too often, people are betrayed by well-meaning but ill-prepared confidants. Worst of all, when your trust has been breached, there's no going back. The information might as well be on the Internet, and your ability to trust someone in the future will be diminished.

If the deepest, most difficult episodes of your life become gossip for your friends, enemies, and casual acquaintances, the betrayal by your confidant will cause damage, which may take years to remedy. Perhaps that relationship may never be repaired. That's why your selection process is so crucial.

Here are some standards:

- You want someone who can listen—really listen. A confidant who constantly interrupts is unacceptable.
- You want someone who is not judgmental. If a person is shocked or offended by what you disclose, that will never work. You need someone who recognizes that he or she is also capable of doing exactly what you've done or worse.
- You want someone who is accepting. If a confidant looks down on you, you know you've chosen the wrong person. Move on to someone who has the character qualities necessary to be understanding and compassionate.
- You want someone who can "feel your pain" and love you in spite of your self-defeating behavior.
- You want someone who will keep your confidence "no matter what." If there's the slightest doubt, don't expose your soul to that person.

We all need at least one such person in our lives, but there are far too few of them available. If you're this kind of person, you have the capacity to help nearly everyone you know. If you're not—and you know you're not—you can see how valuable being this kind of trustworthy confidant can be, can't you?

The good man brings out of his good treasure what is good; and the evil man brings out of his evil treasure what is evil. (MATTHEW 12:35)

Pray: Father, provide me with a person I know I can trust. Help me find a trustworthy person with the capacity to listen.

Write: Spend time with those on your safe list. Do you think they meet the above criteria? If so, go home and write about the time you spent with them. This will help confirm or challenge your impression of them. If you still feel confident about them, take a deep breath. You are ready to proceed.

Reflect
A friend is always loyal,
and a brother is born to help in time of need.
—PROVERBS 17:17 NLT

There are "friends" who destroy each other,
but a real friend sticks closer than a brother.
—PROVERBS 18:24 NLT

The heartfelt counsel of a friend
is as sweet as perfume and incense.
—PROVERBS 27:9 NLT

Breaking Away from Guilt

I will share my experience and my own wrongdoing with a trusted friend, confessing the exact state of my heart.

Read: When you acknowledge the exact nature of your self-defeating behavior, be specific. Be open and be completely forthright. Do your best not to hedge in any way. If you do, it will create disquietude in your soul and be counterproductive. If you're completely forthright, however, the weight of guilt will be broken, freeing you from your encumbrance.

Remember, you are only as sick as your secrets. Once you have confessed them, the burden will be lifted. The shackles will be broken, and you'll be free.

If your behavior has been addictive or habitual, find a support group to help you. There are many available.

Do whatever is necessary to lift the burden of guilt and shame from your life. You've been confined to your emotional prison long enough, and you know it. If you believe you deserve to be shackled, recognize it for what it is—a lie.

God wants you to be free. He is eager to restore you to wholeness, health, peace, and fulfillment.

Shake off your inertia, find a trustworthy friend, schedule a time, and do it. Mustering the courage to actually confess what's troubling you will be difficult, but once you've completed the task, you will be amazed by the relief you experience. It's palpable; there's nothing like it.

If you're reluctant to proceed, it probably means there's something still bothering you. There is something remaining to be uncovered, and it will not leave you alone until you bring it to the light. If necessary, go back to what you wrote throughout step 7 to help you discover what you may not have yet unearthed. Stop hesitating and do it—even if you have to force yourself.

Confess your sins to one another, and pray for one another so that you may be healed. (JAMES 5:16)

Pray: Father, give me the courage to move forward and talk with someone. I'm scared, but I know I need to do it. With your help, I can do it, and I will do it.

Write: Write out what you need to confess. Be very specific. Next, go to your trusted friend and talk it all out. Be thorough.

If that person has not yet emerged, keep praying for God to bring someone into your life. Be on the lookout. God loves to answer prayer, and He will definitely help you find someone trustworthy.

Reflect

He said to them, "Suppose one of you has a friend, and goes to him at midnight and says to him, 'Friend, lend me three loaves; for a friend of mine has come to me from a journey, and I have nothing to set before him'; and from inside he answers and says, 'Do not bother me; the door has already been shut and my children and I are in bed; I cannot get up and give you anything.' I tell you, even though he will not get up and give him anything because he is his friend, yet because of his persistence he will get up and give him as much as he needs.

So I say to you, ask, and it will be given to you; seek, and you will find; knock, and it will be opened to you. For everyone who asks, receives; and he who seeks, finds; and to him who knocks, it will be opened."

—LUKE 11:5–10

You Must Come Clean

I will share my experience and my own wrongdoing with a trusted friend, confessing the exact state of my heart.

Read: After you've confessed your wrongdoing to a trusted friend, prayer is the next step mentioned in James 5:16: "Confess your sins to one another and pray for one another so that you may be healed." The fact that prayer follows confession is not a mistake.

When you expose yourself at the deepest level, becoming completely transparent, the person you confessed to will know how to pray for you. He or she can pray for what you really need and what God really wants for you—deep character transformation. That's why confession is so important. It strengthens the person who makes the confession and the person listening as well.

Confession heals both you and the person you confess to, strengthening the positive character qualities of each. It also makes prayer truly meaningful. Because being transparent with God and with one another has become so rare in our generation, most of our prayers are like the demands of a spoiled four-year-old to an indulgent parent. We pray, "God, give me a new car . . . a new house . . . and, while You're at it, a better job." We want new things, different things, and better things. That's what we pray for—things, things, and more things.

God, on the other hand, is interested in restoring people—hurt, wounded, disillusioned people. People like you and me. Confession and prayer are how He does it, and it's absolutely essential for the quality of your recovery. You must "come clean" before you can become whole.

Pray in the Spirit at all times and on every occasion. Stay alert and be persistent in your prayers for all believers everywhere. (EPHESIANS 6:18 NLT)

166

Pray: Father, teach me how to pray for myself and for others—how to pray for what other people really need rather than for my material enrichment. In light of my confession, teach me to pray more effectively.

Write: After spending time in confession with your trusted friend, ask him or her to pray for you. Do the same for your confidant. Be sure to thank God for His healing power. He is administering it into your life even now—through confession.

Reflect

Be anxious for nothing, but in everything by prayer and supplication with thanksgiving let your requests be made known to God. And the peace of God, which surpasses all comprehension, will guard your hearts and your minds in Christ Jesus.

—PHILIPPIANS 4:6–7

The effective prayer of a righteous man can accomplish much. Elijah was a man with a nature like ours, and he prayed earnestly that it would not rain, and it did not rain on the earth for three years and six months. Then he prayed again, and the sky poured rain and the earth produced its fruit.

—JAMES 5:16–18

An Emotional Tenderizer

I will share my experience and my own wrongdoing with a trusted friend, confessing the exact state of my heart.

Read: In every recovery program, confession is a part of the process, an integral part. Without confession, you will not heal—not completely. You'll remain stuck in a rut, spinning your wheels, getting nowhere.

In recovery from religious abuse, confession is even more important than in other programs. The reason is simple: nearly everybody who has been religiously abused has an issue with pride. Alcoholics, drug addicts, and sex addicts know their behavior is self-defeating, and most of them are not proud of what they've done. If they're candid, they're also ashamed of the pain they've caused others.

It's different for those who have been abused spiritually. The pride factor is much more prevalent. Many say things like the following:

- "I don't have anything to confess. They are the ones who need to confess, not me. I didn't do anything wrong."
- "Okay, I'll confess my part—just as soon as they do and not one minute sooner."
- "God knows everything that happened. I don't need to tell Him anything more. He knows the truth."

Have you ever heard statements like these? Have you ever said them yourself?

I certainly have, and I remember the state of my heart when I did. I was proud. In my woundedness, I was arrogant, self-righteous, and irreconcilable. I didn't realize how callous and bitter I had become. I believed I was okay and everybody else had a problem. For me, pride got in the way of my recovery for a long time.

That's why confession is so important. It's an emotional tenderizer for the heart. It helps take the sting out of the problem, and it's really difficult to stay angry when you finally reach the point where you're willing to open your heart to God.

One more thing—when you tell God what's really going on inside you, He forgives you for all of it. He forgives your bitterness, and He cleanses you from everything that has kept you from living the quality of life you desire.

Confession is simple and easy, but often it's the most difficult thing in the world to do. In the beginning, being humble is always difficult, especially for those of us who are so invested in being right. If you persevere, however, the result will be worth it every time.

If we say that we have fellowship with Him and yet walk in the darkness, we lie and do not practice the truth; but if we walk in the Light as He Himself is in the Light, we have fellowship with one another, and the blood of Jesus His Son cleanses us from all sin. If we say that we have no sin, we are deceiving ourselves, and the truth is not in us. (1 JOHN 1:6–8)

Pray: Father, guide me as I try to be completely honest with You. Enable me to confess my sins to You and a trusted friend. I need Your cleansing, Your strength, and Your restitution.

Write: You have already come a long way in the recovery process. Keep doing the next right thing. Today, consider what the next right thing is for you and spell it out in a sentence or two. Here's a hint: *God wants to change some things in you.* Ask Him to reveal what they might be.

Reflect

Since we have a great High Priest who rules over God's house, let us go right into the presence of God with sincere hearts fully trusting him. For our guilty consciences have been sprinkled with Christ's blood to make us clean, and our bodies have been washed with pure water.

Let us hold tightly without wavering to the hope we affirm, for God can be trusted to keep his promise.

—HEBREWS 10:21–23 NLT

WEEK 10

STEP 9

I humbly ask God to change anything
He desires, and I ask Him to heal my pain.
Because God forgives us as we forgive others,
I forgive my abusers.

Introduction

I humbly ask God to change anything He desires, and I ask Him to heal my pain. Because God forgives us as we forgive others, I forgive my abusers.

Read: Environmentalists inform us that everything we do leaves an imprint on the earth—either positively or negatively, either friendly or unfriendly. It's the same with our relationships. We are either friendly or unfriendly to the people we love and to ourselves. The Scriptures teach that the "sins of the fathers" are passed down through the generations, adversely affecting children, grandchildren, and great-grandchildren.

The tentacles of self-defeating behavior sink deep into the fabric of those we love, and our offspring become just like us in ways we wish they wouldn't. Liars beget deceitful children. Those who have problems with substance abuse are much more likely to have children with similar issues. People with low self-esteem produce like-minded children who become equally defeated in thought and deed.

This is where the value of step 9 really becomes apparent. Because you've been honest about who you are, you are now prepared to break the cycle of self-defeating behavior for yourself and those who follow after you. God wants to heal your pain by transforming it into something positive for every person in your sphere of influence.

Through your honest inventory, you have broken the cords of your emotional chains. Now you are ready to have God make core changes in your character—changes that will leave positive imprints on your offspring. You can begin to lay claim to a brighter future for those who come after you.

Those in your genetic pool either will be blessed or cursed by your life—just as surely as by your carbon imprint. Your impact upon those outside your family is also substantial and equally important. It's why healing the pain from your abuse is so critical.

172

God has the power to make permanent changes in who you are, and He's anxious to do so. By being honest and admitting your culpability rather than continuing to live in denial, you can wipe the slate clean and create a new beginning. You can clean your emotional pool of all pollutants and become a blessing to yourself and to everyone you touch for several generations to come. This is where the fruit of your recovery bears substantive results, where God turns your painful experience into something of incredible value.

The second part of step 9 is the most difficult piece of your recovery process, but it must be done. For you to become everything you believe God intended you to be, you must forgive those who have abused you.

When you do, you'll release yourself to experience the full life your heavenly Father desires for you. That's a promise—a divine promise.

Adversity Makes You Stronger

I humbly ask God to change anything He desires, and I ask Him to heal my pain. Because God forgives us as we forgive others, I forgive my abusers.

Read: Adversity makes you stronger—not a little stronger, but substantially stronger. It's like bodybuilding. Muscles need to be torn down before they can be rebuilt. The Scriptures call this pruning, and God prunes each of His children—some more than others.

I needed pruning, and God is in that business—big time. Once I learned to accept adversity—even welcome it—I began to mature. In my case, I had no alternative. Each situation made me a little more of who I am today. None of it was easy. It was difficult and it continues to be difficult, but the end result was worth it. It will also be worth it for you. It's what makes you more fruitful and capable of living a more fulfilled life.

When adversity comes, stop, reflect, and align your reactions with what you know God wants you to do. Refuse to retreat into self-defeating behavior, which will undermine your growth. Reject the darkness and its binding chains at all costs.

If you do, your character will be strengthened—regardless of the situation—and proven character has incredible value. It's worth more than silver or gold.

God wants to make changes in you, and He's determined to accomplish His goal. The changes you experience are the blessing that emerges from the adversity you've experienced. Learn to embrace it rather than resent it. If you do, its debilitating pain will begin to heal. One day, you'll think about it, and the pain will be gone. In its place will be a valuable learning experience, which will enrich your life and the lives of everyone around you.

In my case, my abuse resulted in invaluable character growth. Because

I know this truth with absolute certainty, I do not regret the past—nor do I want to close the door on it. My experiences have left me richer in character than I ever dreamed possible. I'm not diminished by them, nor am I bitter or resentful. On the contrary, they have given me the insight and understanding I've always wanted but was never able to obtain. For that, I'm truly grateful.

> *We can rejoice, too, when we run into problems and trials, for we know that they help us develop endurance. And endurance develops strength of character, and character strengthens our confident hope of salvation. And this hope will not lead to disappointment. For we know how dearly God loves us, because he has given us the Holy Spirit to fill our hearts with his love.* (ROMANS 5:3–5 NLT)

Pray: Father, enable me to embrace my adversity rather than deny it or run from it. Help me see it as You see it—as an opportunity for growth. Without You working in me, I can't imagine this being possible.

Write: What will it take for you to accept—and even welcome—adversity in your life rather than dread it or run away from it? Talk to God about it, and journal your feelings.

Reflect

> *We know that God causes all things to work together for good to those who love God, to those who are called according to His purpose.*
> —ROMANS 8:28

> *God has now revealed to us his mysterious plan regarding Christ, a plan to fulfill his own good pleasure. And this is the plan: At the right time he will bring everything together under the authority of Christ— everything in heaven and on earth. Furthermore, because we are united with Christ, we have received an inheritance from God, for he chose us in advance, and he makes everything work out according to his plan.*
> —EPHESIANS 1:9–11 NLT

Your Pain Has Value

I humbly ask God to change anything He desires, and I ask Him to heal my pain. Because God forgives us as we forgive others, I forgive my abusers.

Read: I've consistently maintained that exposing the truth to the light will set you free—the truth about your abuse and the truth about who you really are. I believe this with all of my heart.

For me, a blessing has resulted from each of my painful experiences. None has weakened me. I'm stronger because of each disappointing failure—not the other way around.

It can be the same for you. All you have to do is acknowledge who you really are and allow God to change you.

I know who I am more completely than I ever have, and I like who I am. I'm no longer ashamed of myself or of my actions. Those who sought to destroy me by being abusive failed to achieve their goal. I'm stronger than I've ever been. I'm also more resilient. God reached into the pit—into the cesspool—and pulled me out so that I could tell you that you have hope, that you have a future. What my abusers meant for evil, God meant for good. It can be the same for you. My pain had purpose; so has yours—all of it.

My story may be complex, but the good that resulted from my pain is simple. God used it to shape me into a man of proven character. Every dramatic event, including my religious abuse, was a part of making that happen. It has made me a useful person, but it required decades.

You can have the same experience. While you are in the valley of despair, you can see God's hand and loving guidance. These are not always as obvious while you're on the mountaintop of joy. God wants to transform you from the inside out. After two months of work, you're now at the threshold of making that change a reality.

All you have to do is permit God to change anything He wants. When you do, your value will increase exponentially as rich character qualities will be solidified in you. Your surrender to God will also provide the healing for your soul that has eluded you for so long.

> *I waited patiently for the LORD to help me,*
>   *and he turned to me and heard my cry.*
> *He lifted me out of the pit of despair,*
>   *out of the mud and the mire.*
> *He set my feet on solid ground*
>   *and steadied me as I walked along.*
> *He has given me a new song to sing,*
>   *a hymn of praise to our God.* (PSALM 40:1–3 NLT)

Pray: Father, I want to give You permission to make whatever changes You desire in my life, but I need your strength to truly turn this control over to You. Without Your help, I'll fall back into my old patterns. I know I will. Help me avoid this trap.

Write: God can be trusted. He is powerful, but He also is very, very good. Keeping this in mind, take time to write any reservations you may have about allowing Him to make core changes in you. You must be completely honest with yourself and with God on this matter.

Reflect

> *"I know the plans that I have for you," declares the LORD, "plans for welfare and not for calamity to give you a future and a hope."*
>   —JEREMIAH 29:11

> *Joseph said to them, "Do not be afraid, for am I in God's place? As for you, you meant evil against me, but God meant it for good in order to bring about this present result, to preserve many people alive. So therefore, do not be afraid; I will provide for you and your little ones." So he comforted them and spoke kindly to them.*
>   —GENESIS 50:19–21

Purpose Behind the Pain

I humbly ask God to change anything He desires, and I ask Him to heal my pain. Because God forgives us as we forgive others, I forgive my abusers.

Read: Recognizing the value of your painful, abusive experience may be very difficult, but it's there, awaiting discovery. You simply have to search for it—as you would a misplaced piece of valuable jewelry. Like lost jewelry, it never should be far from your mind. When you find it, your relief and joy will be just as rewarding. You will have found something of significant value, something to treasure.

For me, each tumultuous, life-altering event seemed random for a long time, but it all began to come together when I learned to be fully attuned to life. That happened when I stopped living on the borders of consciousness, medicating my pain and my problems rather than facing them. That's why sobriety has been so important for me. I used alcohol to medicate my pain, which it did, but it also clouded my judgment as well as my perception of reality.

I needed to think soberly. When I mastered the steps to make that a reality, the patterns emerged—slowly, to be sure—but inevitably. I began to understand the purpose behind each difficult situation. I finally "got" the lesson I was supposed to learn. Without sobriety, I never would have been able to discern my distorted perspective from the truth. I had to abandon my self-defeating behavior—just like you do.

When I did, truth began to enlighten me, providing the freedom to cast aside my debilitating manacles. Without the shackles, I was free to embrace a life of proactive forthrightness—a life full of love, joy, and peace. These inestimable character qualities are what I exchanged for resentment and an unforgiving heart. By nurturing my bitterness, I thought I was punishing my abusers, but I was only punishing myself, spinning my wheels purposelessly for years.

God wants to free you from your debilitating past—just like He did with me. All you have to do is ask. When you do, He will be free to change your attitude, change your behavior, and change your heart.

> *Keep on asking, and you will receive what you ask for. Keep on seeking, and you will find. Keep on knocking, and the door will be opened to you. For everyone who asks, receives. Everyone who seeks, finds. And to everyone who knocks, the door will be opened.* (MATTHEW 7:7–8 NLT)

Pray: Father, I do want to be free from the past and from all of the pain it causes. Heal me from any lingering shame, anger, and bitterness. Please come in and make any changes necessary to make my healing real and permanent.

Write: Ask God to make these changes, and then be patient. For greater clarity about the changes you desire to be made, describe in writing exactly what you want. Keep in mind that God knows what changes need to be made in your life and when. Your responsibility is to ask for them. God's responsibility is to make them when He chooses to do so.

Reflect

> *The Lord is the Spirit, and wherever the Spirit of the Lord is, there is freedom So all of us who have had that veil removed can see and reflect the glory of the Lord. And the Lord—who is the Spirit—makes us more and more like him as we are changed into his glorious image.*
> —2 CORINTHIANS 3:17–18 NLT

Setting Yourself Free

I humbly ask God to change anything He desires, and I ask Him to heal my pain. Because God forgives us as we forgive others, I forgive my abuser.

Read: When you stop blaming people and circumstances for your lot in life, you come to the threshold of wisdom—God's wisdom. When you begin to think soberly rather than through a self-centered prism, you recognize that God works everything to your good (see Romans 8:29), including your abuse. This is not to say that God intended or purposed your abuse, but He can take your situation and bring good out of it.

At some point, you may come to understand how God has brought good from your situation. Many people do. Perhaps you already understand some aspects of it.

Even if you don't, you can count on God's character. Although He didn't cause your abuse, you realize He can bring blessings from it. You can also know that God is always working on your behalf—that He wants to heal you at the core of your being. He wants to free you from each chain that binds you.

By embracing gratitude rather than resentment, it's much easier to develop an attitude of forgiveness. By forgiving others, you will be setting yourself free.

That's correct. You will set yourself free, not your abuser. Being resentful doesn't hurt your abuser; it hurts you. In essence, it's like saying, "I'll get even with you. I'll hurt *me*." That's what resentment and unforgiveness do. They hurt the person who has been abused, not the abuser.

The person set free by forgiveness is you. When you realize you are only hurting yourself and prolonging your recovery by nurturing anger and bitterness, doesn't it make sense to let them go? Why would you want to nurture toxic emotions and attitudes, which do nothing positive or constructive for you? Why would you stay in an emotional prison one additional day when it's in your power to set yourself free?

Go ahead and do it. Forgive your abusers as you trust God to give you a forgiving heart for each one.

It was for freedom that Christ set us free. (GALATIANS 5:1)

Pray: Father, I forgive my abusers once and for all. I let go of my unforgiveness totally, knowing that once I have done so, it's forgiven completely—just like You've forgiven me. Please open my eyes to understand how to forgive from Your perspective.

Write: When you forgive your abusers, you can replace resentment with gratitude. Take time to come up with a list of all the things in your life for which you are grateful. Once you complete the initial list, add five more items every day for the next two weeks. Add to this list before the end of each day. There is power in being grateful. Gratitude has no downside.

Reflect

Beyond all these things put on love, which is the perfect bond of unity. Let the peace of Christ rule in your hearts, to which indeed you were called in one body; and be thankful. Let the word of Christ richly dwell within you, with all wisdom teaching and admonishing one another with psalms and hymns and spiritual songs, singing with thankfulness in your hearts to God. Whatever you do in word or deed, do all in the name of the Lord Jesus, giving thanks through Him to God the Father.

—COLOSSIANS 3:14–17

*I will give thanks to You, O Lord my God, with all my heart,
    And will glorify Your name forever.
For Your loving kindness toward me is great,
    And You have delivered my soul from the depths of Sheol.*

—PSALM 86:12–13

Forgiving Your Abuser

I humbly ask God to change anything He desires, and I ask Him to heal my pain. Because God forgives us as we forgive others, I forgive my abusers.

Read: In the depths of despair, you can learn—really learn—about life and who you are. When you've been crushed, ridiculed, and discarded, all pretentiousness leaves you. You cease being puffed up and arrogant. You become reduced to practically nothing emotionally, and your heart is broken. Even your countenance seems to diminish as self-pity consumes you—at least for a while.

Before your world came crashing down, you thought you had something significant to offer. God needed you—not the other way around. You were important; you brought something to the table. Although you never would admit it publicly, you probably thought you were better than most. You thought you were so attuned to God that your thoughts were His thoughts or at least close to them. You were a person of consequence—more significant than your peers.

This is the mind-set of those capable of being spiritually abusive. This is what they believe, and it's why they are capable of such cruelty in the name of God. Even if you never have been abusive to someone, in the back of your mind, you've probably entertained these thoughts.

After your abuse, you no longer consider such grandiose thoughts, do you? Your experience has changed all of that. In fact, isn't it exactly the opposite?

Your heavenly Father has allowed you to be stripped of all pretentiousness. Now that you've bottomed out and have come so far in your recovery, doesn't this abusive mind-set seem misguided, superficial, and even a little pitiful? When you look at it like it really is, doesn't refusing to forgive someone who is so limited seem beneath you? Is it worth staying emotionally imprisoned just to harbor anger against someone who is clearly misguided?

Of course, it isn't. That's why you should take the final step and forgive your abuser. Just let it go—let it all go. Forgive the abuser once and for all.

When you do, you will release yourself to experience the abundance God has for you. If you refuse, you'll continue to be tied to your abuser in unhealthy ways. The choice, as always, is yours.

Let all bitterness and wrath and anger and clamor and slander be put away from you, along with all malice. Be kind to one another, tenderhearted, forgiving each other, just as God in Christ also has forgiven you. (EPHESIANS 4:31–32)

Pray: God, I want to be free from the unforgiveness I have nurtured for so long. I do forgive my abusers. Please change my heart, and never allow bitterness to rule it again.

Write: Forgiveness is not based on a feeling, but on a choice. Today choose to forgive those who have harmed you. Write the name down of every person you choose to forgive. The emotional release will follow eventually, but the choice to forgive must come first. Talk to God about this process, and ask Him for His power to make the choice to forgive.

Reflect

How blessed is he whose transgression is forgiven,
    Whose sin is covered!
How blessed is the man to whom the LORD does not impute iniquity,
    And in whose spirit there is no deceit!
When I kept silent about my sin, my body wasted away
    Through my groaning all day long.
For day and night Your hand was heavy upon me;
    My vitality was drained away as with the fever heat of summer.
I acknowledged my sin to You,
    And my iniquity I did not hide;
    I said, "I will confess my transgressions to the LORD";
    And You forgave the guilt of my sin.

—PSALM 32:1–5

As We Forgive Others

I humbly ask God to change anything He desires, and I ask Him to heal my pain. Because God forgives us as we forgive others, I forgive my abusers.

Read: There's a final piece to the forgiveness puzzle, a piece that is critical. When you hold on to unforgiveness, when you refuse to release your blame and your bitterness, you hurt yourself more than you realize. In the Lord's Prayer, Jesus says, "Forgive us our sins, as we have forgiven those who sin against us" (Matthew 6:12 NLT).

In order to wipe your slate clean, you must forgive those who have sinned against you, those who have abused you. Refusing to forgive your abusers keeps you tied to them in an endless cycle of anger, resentment, blame, bitterness, and nearly every other negative emotion you can experience.

When you do forgive them, when you let it all go, everything changes. You invite forgiveness for yourself as well. This is when God takes the guilt of your self-defeating behavior and remembers it no more. Although the consequences of your behavior remain, He sends your guilt as far as the east is from the west. This is when you allow God to heal you completely.

There's no downside to forgiveness. It isn't being weak; it's being strong. Only a strong person is capable of forgiveness. Weak people don't have enough character to forsake their right to be victims. They don't own enough of their souls to do it. They have to keep the bitterness and resentment churning, clinging to it desperately. It provides nourishment and purpose for their unfulfilled existence. At least, they believe it does.

By forgiving your abusers, you are choosing freedom and life. Don't continue to be imprisoned one day further. Choose to forgive all of it. It's not only the right thing to do, but it will also provide health to your soul, enriching you with such positive character qualities as joy, peace, and kindness.

> He has removed our sins as far from us
>   as the east is from the west.
> The LORD is like a father to his children,
>   tender and compassionate to those who fear him. (PSALM 103:12–13 NLT)

Pray: Father, give me the strength to forgive those who have wronged me. Let me do so completely. Let this be the last time I ever need to address this subject with You. Let it end here—once and for all.

Write: Keep in mind that forgiveness is *not* making excuses for the person who has hurt you. It's *not* denial or making light of the wrong that has been done. It's saying, "I know what you have done, and I choose to let it go and not hold it against you any longer." It is a deliberate and conscious choice you have within your power to make.

Is there anything still standing in your way to forgive? If so, journal about whatever is holding you back. Remember, freedom's doorway is just on the other side of forgiveness.

Reflect

> If you forgive others for their transgressions, your heavenly Father will also forgive you. But if you do not forgive others, then your Father will not forgive your transgressions.
>
> —MATTHEW 6:14–15

> Let all bitterness and wrath and anger and clamor and slander be put away from you, along with all malice. Be kind to one another, tender-hearted, forgiving each other, just as God in Christ also has forgiven you.
>
> —EPHESIANS 4:31–32

WEEK 11

STEP 10

I choose to believe God still has a purpose for
my life—a purpose for good and not evil.

Introduction

I choose to believe God still has a purpose for my life—a purpose for good and not evil.

No matter how far down the road to destruction you have traveled, you can choose to turn your life around. As long as there is breath in your lungs, you can return to a loving God—a God who will welcome you back with open arms. You can choose God's way over self-defeating behavior. You can choose:

- love over hate
- forgiveness over retaliation
- faith over fear
- joy over depression
- peace over turmoil
- reconciliation over alienation

You can choose right over wrong. You can abandon a half-life of self-pity and embrace a life filled with purpose and enhanced character development. You can stop feeling sorry for yourself and become everything God ever intended you to be. You have this power; the choice is yours.

God still has a purpose for your life. You can count on it. Think of the life of John Newton who wrote "Amazing Grace." Although he was a slave trader tormenting thousands, he turned his life around, and the product of his transformation has blessed every generation for more than two hundred years. It's hard to think of someone whose life could have more extremes than his. The destruction he inflicted on those sold into slavery was catastrophic.

Once he realized the error of his ways and made a decision to change course, however, his impact was just as transforming—but for good. He discovered who he was, and he made a commitment to change. So can you.

You have the same power. It starts with being transparent and believing God still has a purpose for your life—a purpose for good and not for destruction. If you understand this and accept it as true, you will unleash the power of Almighty God to transform your life. This demonstrable truth is not an exaggeration.

The positive purpose for your life still lies ahead, not behind. You can be a blessing to everyone you touch, including those you've harmed along the way. Your slate is clean through the recovery you've already accomplished, and the future holds great promise. It's why your recovery is so important and the specific purpose for step 10.

Faith or Sentimental Drivel?

I choose to believe God still has a purpose for my life—a purpose for good and not evil.

Read: When circumstances are particularly difficult, how many times have you heard someone say, "It'll be okay. You just need to have a little faith. Everything will work out for the best"?

People mean well when they make such statements, but it really doesn't help. In fact, if you're like me, it makes you want to scream, or worse. It's more like a pathetic sentiment than something real and tangible, and pathetic sentiments can't help when you need real answers to difficult problems.

At the same time, having faith is exactly what you need when you have no answers and everything looks bleak. But real faith is not, in the least, the sentimental drivel most consider it to be. It's absolute confidence and total assurance that God is active and in charge of the future. He knows every aspect of your situation, and He already has everything worked out. There is nothing you can tell God that He doesn't already know. He's got your back.

If you believe this and can base your confidence upon it, if you know it's more tangible than the ground you're walking upon, then you can say: "I know whom I believe in, and I'm convinced He is able to take care of me in whatever situation I'm in. Nothing can pry me from His grasp."

That's real faith, and its value is priceless. It's what God is after in you and why your recovery is so valuable to him.

Faith is the confidence that what we hope for will actually happen; it gives us assurance about things we cannot see. (HEBREWS 11:1 NLT)

Pray: Father, I know my faith is not as strong as it needs to be. Help develop real faith in me. Enable me to believe in Your power and goodness. Thank You for being so trustworthy and so good.

Write: Take some time to reflect about who God is and what He has revealed about your life. You do have meaning, and He does have a purpose for everything you've encountered or ever will encounter. Journal about the real answers you need to the real problems you are currently facing. Remember, no problem is too big or too complex for God.

Reflect

Jesus answered and said to them, "Truly I say to you, if you have faith and do not doubt, you will not only do what was done to the fig tree, but even if you say to this mountain, 'Be taken up and cast into the sea,' it will happen. And all things you ask in prayer, believing, you will receive."

—MATTHEW 21:21–22

I have been crucified with Christ; and it is no longer I who live, but Christ lives in me; and the life which I now live in the flesh I live by faith in the Son of God, who loved me and gave Himself up for me.

—GALATIANS 2:20

The Way We Were

I choose to believe God still has a purpose for my life—a purpose for good and not evil.

Read: As I walked through the magnificent city of Florence—*Firenza* in Italiano—evidence of Christian civilization was everywhere. I visited a church built in the fifth century. In other churches I saw artifacts of medieval and Renaissance architecture everywhere, as well as priceless works of art. It was truly magnificent.

The entire city was like a museum—an appropriate metaphor for the reality of Florentine life in the twenty-first century. The glory of Christianity was ubiquitous, but it was entirely from the past. This gave me pause to think about my walk with the Lord.

God has had His hand on my life for decades, but I wondered if there was any current evidence of it. I wondered if all that was left was similar to Florence—a museum of what God had done in the past.

Although I'm grateful for what He has accomplished in me, neither my life nor yours is meant to be a museum. Because God is alive and active, our lives must bear the fruit of His nature and not be a museum of what we once were but are no longer. As I thought about this, I meditated on the Scripture passage quoted below:

> *The word of God is living and active and sharper than any two-edged sword, and piercing as far as the division of soul and spirit, of both joints and marrow, and able to judge the thoughts and intentions of the heart. And there is no creature hidden from His sight, but all things are open and laid bare to the eyes of Him with whom we have to do.* (HEBREWS 4:12–13)

Pray: Father, I want my relationship with You to be alive and active—not a relic of the past or a distant memory. If needed, move me out of my comfort zone and give me a passion to know You more fully.

Write: Write about how to connect with God at a deeper, more active level, Then write about what actions you would undertake to make this a reality. Write down one thing you can do this week that will deepen your relationship with Him. Now go and do it.

Reflect

Abide in Me, and I in you. As the branch cannot bear fruit of itself unless it abides in the vine, so neither can you unless you abide in Me. I am the vine, you are the branches; he who abides in Me and I in him, he bears much fruit, for apart from Me you can do nothing.

—JOHN 15:4–5

For this reason also, since the day we heard of it, we have not ceased to pray for you and to ask that you may be filled with the knowledge of His will in all spiritual wisdom and understanding, so that you will walk in a manner worthy of the Lord, to please Him in all respects, bearing fruit in every good work and increasing in the knowledge of God; strengthened with all power, according to His glorious might, for the attaining of all steadfastness and patience; joyously giving thanks to the Father, who has qualified us to share in the inheritance of the saints in Light.

—COLOSSIANS 1:9–12

As Good as It Gets?

I choose to believe God still has a purpose for my life—a purpose for good and not evil.

Read: *If a man is going to do anything worthwhile, there are times when he has to risk everything on his leap, and in the spiritual domain, Jesus Christ demands that you risk everything you hold by common sense and leap into what He says, and immediately you do, you find that what He says fits on as solidly as common sense* (Oswald Chambers).

Going through an abusive situation is never something a person plans or invites into his or her life. When it happens, it's always an unexpected detour. It's surprising and definitely unwanted.

At the same time, God can be counted on to bring purpose out of the chaos, including undesirable situations—even abusive situations. If we learn to believe that God is still in charge and has a positive plan for our lives, we are on the right track.

It's normal to go through a myriad of emotions after being abused, including every stage of grief, but at the other end, we must come to the point where we are willing to risk it all again. We must learn that God still has us in the palm of His hand and nothing can separate us from His love. Nothing can thwart His ultimate purpose.

God is keen on the idea of our being everything He wants us to be. Developing rich character qualities in us like love, joy, peace, patience, and kindness is always the end result He desires. Knowing God is with you, regardless of the situation, makes trusting Him your wisest option—even after your abusive experience.

For I am convinced that neither death, nor life, nor angels, nor principalities, nor things present, nor things to come, nor powers, nor height, nor depth, nor any other created thing, will be able to separate us from the love of God, which is in Christ Jesus our Lord. (ROMANS 8:38–39)

Pray: Father, enable me to believe You still have a positive plan for my life—a plan for good things and not bad.

Write: Try to find and talk to others who have been through religious abuse. There are millions of them. Knowing what others are facing—or have faced—can aid your recovery greatly. You are not alone—not even close. Write about what you discover in these conversations.

Reflect
> Let the wicked change their ways
>   and banish the very thought of doing wrong.
> Let them turn to the LORD that he may have mercy on them.
>   Yes, turn to our God, for he will forgive generously.

> "My thoughts are nothing like your thoughts," says the LORD.
>   "And my ways are far beyond anything you could imagine.
> For just as the heavens are higher than the earth,
>   so my ways are higher than your ways
>   and my thoughts higher than your thoughts."

—ISAIAH 55:7–9 NLT

As He Sees Fit

I choose to believe God still has a purpose for my life—a purpose for good and not evil.

Read: When I think of the Easter season and the events leading to the death of Jesus, I definitely can identify with when Christ asked if there was any way He could accomplish the Father's will without suffering crucifixion. When I was younger, this didn't seem significant, but as I've matured, it's something I think about quite often.

I want my life to be easier. Obviously, there's no real comparison between my difficulties and dying for the sins of mankind, but being faithful to God's will isn't easy—no matter who you are.

The Scriptures teach that nothing beyond our capacity is ever put upon us. I know that's true, but it seems God has a much higher view of my capacity than I do. He stretches me repeatedly, and most of the time, I wish He wouldn't. I want Him to use me but in a nice way—not in a difficult way where my limitations are exposed.

Frankly, I'd settle for a year or two of the easy life, wouldn't you? But that's not going to happen, and I know it. It's just wishful thinking.

Because God has a huge investment in each of us, He has determined to use us as He sees fit. It's why we can have joy even when there's substantial sadness in our lives. Our travails have value and purpose. When circumstances look bleak, comfort yourself with the assurance of this truth.

We can rejoice, too, when we run into problems and trials, for we know that they help us develop endurance. And endurance develops strength of character, and character strengthens our confident hope of salvation. And this hope will not lead to disappointment. For we know how dearly God loves us, because he has given us the Holy Spirit to fill our hearts with his love. (ROMANS 5:3–5 NLT)

Pray: Lord, I am thankful You want to use me, but it is hard to deal with what I have to face in my life. Give me the ability to persevere and give glory to You in the midst of each taxing circumstance.

Write: Consider what God is doing in your life. He uses your past, your present, your joys, and your failures to shape you into the person He wants you to be. He even uses your dreams and desires to lead you where you can make a difference in the world. Take time to journal about where you think God might be leading you. What might His purpose be for the rest of your life?

Reflect

Just as the sufferings of Christ are ours in abundance, so also our comfort is abundant through Christ. But if we are afflicted, it is for your comfort and salvation; or if we are comforted, it is for your comfort, which is effective in the patient enduring of the same sufferings which we also suffer; and our hope for you is firmly grounded, knowing that as you are sharers of our sufferings, so also you are sharers of our comfort.

—2 CORINTHIANS 1:5–7

Things Didn't Go Well

I choose to believe God still has a purpose for my life—a purpose for good and not evil.

Read: A critical part of your recovery is developing a stronger, more resilient mind-set. Too often, people talk about the joys of being a Christian, but when adversity comes, they fall apart and complain about how hard life is. The question that needs answering is this: *why shouldn't it be hard?*

God allowed His Son to go through humiliation, gruesome torture, and death. Things didn't go well for Jesus, and His all-powerful Father just sat by and allowed it to happen—without rescuing Him. It's what we celebrate at Easter: Christ's crucifixion, death, and resurrection. We plan activities during Easter week, but for most of us, we never really consider the purpose of taking up our crosses—as Jesus did—and following Him.

Instead we whine and complain that things should be going better for us. We want the burdens of our problems taken away or at least mitigated, believing it's God's responsibility to calm the waters in our lives. It never occurs to us that the strain of life makes us stronger and has incredible value. What we consider a burden or a hindrance is of priceless value to our heavenly Father.

We want to walk with the Lord, just as long as it's easy, conflict free, and politically correct. When it isn't, we either buckle under the prevailing culture or complain so much we miss the value of the lesson.

We look at the idea of adversity, which is integral to Christianity, as abnormal and a sign that our walk must be flawed. This simply isn't true, and it's not taught in the New Testament. To learn the lesson from your abuse, you must recognize that it is an expected part of this life.

That I may know Him and the power of His resurrection and the fellowship of His sufferings, being conformed to His death; in order that I may attain to the resurrection from the dead. (PHILIPPIANS 3:10–11)

Pray: God, help me understand that You can bring good out of all the difficulties I've had in life—even my abuse. Enable me to believe You still have a plan and a purpose for me. Help me walk by Your faith and not by my sight.

Write: Reflect on your life before the abuse occurred. Can you recognize how God was working even in the hard times before your abuse? Often you need to be outside of the circumstances to get a clear view. Write down these times—as well as how God used them in your life. Also stretch yourself and write down how God has used your religious abuse for good. Remember, nothing in our lives is without purpose.

Reflect

I consider that the sufferings of this present time are not worthy to be compared with the glory that is to be revealed to us. For the anxious longing of the creation waits eagerly for the revealing of the sons of God.

—ROMANS 8:18–19

Beloved, do not be surprised at the fiery ordeal among you, which comes upon you for your testing, as though some strange thing were happening to you; but to the degree that you share the sufferings of Christ, keep on rejoicing, so that also at the revelation of His glory you may rejoice with exultation.

—1 PETER 4:12–13

Renewing Your Mind

I choose to believe God still has a purpose for my life—a purpose for good and not evil.

Read: When a person is abused verbally, feelings of worthlessness and low self-esteem are inevitable. These feelings are even more pronounced when the abuse comes from a spiritual leader. That's because the abusee's relationship with God comes into question as well. Essentially, the abuser is saying, "You're not okay, and your relationship with God is not okay either."

The devastation caused by such an internalized message is incalculable. The hardest thing in the world for abused people to do is believe God still loves them—that He considers them to be worthwhile. They are emotionally unable to accept the positive, validating things God has to say about them in the Scriptures. Somehow it doesn't seem to apply to them. In the back of their minds, they accept what the abusive person has said about them as true: that they are indeed unworthy.

Spiritual leaders are there to lead, and when they use their power destructively, they still lead—just in a direction that adversely affects the follower. The emotional impact upon the person is just as strong, maybe stronger, as it penetrates the soul with its message of condemnation. The abusee internalizes the message that he or she has committed an unpardonable sin with devastating consequences.

This is why abused people need to work at recovery. Step 10 is specifically about renewing your mind to believe God still has a purpose for your life—a plan for good things and not bad things. No matter how devastated and defeated you've become, the power to be a dynamic, worthwhile person is still there—available for the asking. The Scriptures provide this promise: "I am convinced that neither death, nor life, nor angels, nor principalities, nor things present, nor things to come, nor powers, nor height, nor depth, nor any other created thing, will be able to separate us from the love of God, which is in Christ Jesus our Lord" (Romans 8:38–39).

Either this is true or it isn't. Either you can believe what the Scriptures say or what your abusers have said. If you choose to accept what God has said as true, you are on your way to renewing your mind. You are on your way to recovery.

Do not be conformed to this world, but be transformed by the renewing of your mind, so that you may prove what the will of God is, that which is good and acceptable and perfect. (ROMANS 12:2)

Pray: Father, show me how to renew my mind and accept that what You have said is true. Help me see what my abusers have said about me for what it is—a lie. Thank You for Your goodness and for continuing to love me just the way I am.

Write: Think back through your journey—especially the work you completeted in step 4. Take time to journal about your recovery and what you don't want to forget while in the recovery process. In the areas where you are weak, don't beat yourself up with criticism. Instead, redouble your efforts in those areas. It will make you much stronger.

If you're still having trouble accepting God's promises as true, return to step 4 and take a look at the work you did six weeks ago.

Reflect

You have not received a spirit of slavery leading to fear again, but you have received a spirit of adoption as sons by which we cry out, "Abba! Father!" The Spirit Himself testifies with our spirit that we are children of God, and if children, heirs also, heirs of God and fellow heirs with Christ, if indeed we suffer with Him so that we may also be glorified with Him.

—ROMANS 8:15–17

We know that God causes all things to work together for good to those who love God, to those who are called according to His purpose. For those whom He foreknew, He also predestined to become conformed to the image of His Son, so that He would be the firstborn among many brethren; and these whom He predestined, He also called; and these whom He called, He also justified; and these whom He justified, He also glorified.

What then shall we say to these things? If God is for us, who is against us?

—ROMANS 8:28–31

WEEK 12

STEP 11

I make a commitment to nurture my relationship
with God, asking Him to reveal His will to me and
to give me the power to carry it out.

Introduction

I make a commitment to nurture my relationship with God, asking Him to reveal His will to me and to give me the power to carry it out.

Once you are no longer angry with God nor blame Him for your abuse, you will begin to see life more clearly—from a healthier, more accurate perspective. Then, when you least expect it, it will happen. It will probably just pass through your mind like a zephyr, like a gentle breeze of illumination that penetrates your soul.

Intuitively, you'll know the Holy Spirit is renewing your mind and your heart, providing wisdom. Everything will finally come together. When this occurs—and it will—you'll be undone. Instantly, you'll realize precisely how much God loves you; and this realization will be overwhelming. From that precise moment, everything inside you will change and you'll never be the same again—not if you live to be ninety.

You will become aware of your value to God and what it cost Him to make you His own. You'll know—perhaps for the first time—the depth of God's love and how safe you are in the hands of the Master. At that moment, nothing else will matter. Neither self-fulfillment nor material comforts will seem important.

That's when God's wisdom will enter your heart, and you will be changed from the inside out. It's your Mount of Transfiguration, the place where you cannot sing "Amazing Grace" without weeping from heartfelt gratitude, knowing that the "wretch" described in the song is you.

Suddenly, everything will become clear; and you'll know your life still has value and purpose. This moment may not last long, but it doesn't matter. You've seen reality—if only for an instant—the way God sees it, and nothing will ever be the same again. The purpose for your recovery will start to come together. You'll look at your past differently—with more clarity.

Your abusers had a purpose—to use you and to thoroughly exploit you. Then, when they were through, they discarded you as someone no longer worth their time or trouble. For a while, maybe even for years, your lifestyle validated their assessment as you pursued self-defeating behavior. But now that your eyes have been opened, those days can be over and need never return.

What your abuser used to destroy you, God has used to rebuild you—from the inside out. When this reality dawns on you, when you truly understand, you will begin to grasp God's love—a love that cannot be shaken or diminished. Once you understand this, like the phoenix, you will rise out of the ashes—out of your doldrums—to newness of life. You will be a better person than ever before, and you'll be thankful. It's been worth it—all of it, including your abusive experience. That's when you'll eagerly embrace step 11.

Witnessing . . . the Right Way

I make a commitment to nurture my relationship with God, asking Him to reveal His will to me and to give me the power to carry it out.

Read: I remember when I first invited Christ into my life as a sophomore in college through the ministry of Campus Crusade for Christ. Witnessing was the most important aspect of this ministry, and I dutifully walked up and down the beaches of Southern California—proselytizing. It's what we did—for fun.

I never really liked intruding on people who were there to enjoy a relaxing afternoon, but I was determined to be a great Campus Crusader. I convinced dozens of people to pray with me to invite Christ into their lives. Reflecting back decades later, I wonder how much of this exercise was real. I suspect I was better at imposing my will upon them than any of them were at surrendering their wills to God. I never saw any of them again, and I now consider my efforts to have been largely futile.

Forty years later, I was working out at the YMCA in my continuous struggle to maintain a semblance of fitness. As I was walking to the water fountain, an older woman, who I did not know but had seen repeatedly for years, stopped me. She asked if I would donate a copy of my book *Hi, My Name Is Jack* to the library at the Jewish retirement library she managed. The book is my story, my testimony, and is based on the kind of rigorous honesty you would expect from someone in recovery.

As you might expect, I told her I would. As I drove home, I thought my witness to her might have been more effective than anything I ever did on the beaches in my evangelistic fervor as a youth. While at the YMCA, she saw something in me worth sharing with hundreds of Jewish retirees. My witness, in this case, actually may help someone because it was focused on "walking the walk" and not "talking the talk." Best of all, I never said a word. It was completely based on my behavior—my daily actions witnessed by her, which made it truly gratifying.

> *The people who influence us most are not those who buttonhole us and talk to us but those who live their lives like the stars in the heaven and the lilies in the field, perfectly simple and unaffectedly. Those are the lives that mold us.* (OSWALD CHAMBERS)

> *Do everything without complaining and arguing, so that no one can criticize you. Live clean, innocent lives as children of God, shining like bright lights in a world full of crooked and perverse people.* (PHILIPPIANS 2:14–15 NLT)

Pray: Lord, teach me to live my life unaffectedly—just like a child who is completely secure in the love of a benevolent parent. Let my strong relationship with You be a witness to all who know me. Help me walk the walk and not simply talk the talk. Help me keep my eyes constantly on You.

Write: What might it look like for you to be a witness for Christ? Take time to journal your answer. Be specific. Now ask God what He thinks about your being a witness to others who have been abused.

Reflect

> *Since we have so great a cloud of witnesses surrounding us, let us also lay aside every encumbrance and the sin which so easily entangles us, and let us run with endurance the race that is set before us, fixing our eyes on Jesus, the author and perfecter of faith, who for the joy set before Him endured the cross, despising the shame, and has sat down at the right hand of the throne of God.*
>
> *For consider Him who has endured such hostility by sinners against Himself, so that you will not grow weary and lose heart.*
>
> —HEBREWS 12:1–3

> *He said to them, "It is not for you to know times or epochs which the Father has fixed by His own authority; but you will receive power when the Holy Spirit has come upon you; and you shall be My*

witnesses both in Jerusalem, and in all Judea and Samaria, and even to the remotest part of the earth."

And after He had said these things, He was lifted up while they were looking on, and a cloud received Him out of their sight.

—ACTS 1:7–9

Love One Another

I make a commitment to nurture my relationship with God, asking Him to reveal His will to me and to give me the power to carry it out.

Read: I always find it interesting when someone says, "Have you been witnessing for the Lord lately?" At thousands of churches across America, this question is asked repeatedly by well-meaning pastors and evangelistic leaders. Although they may think the question is an encouragement to "speak out boldly," it usually has the opposite effect.

Actually, it's intimidating and produces fear, guilt, and shame in the heart of the hearer—sometimes paralyzing the person with fear. More important, it's the wrong question to ask. It implies that force-feeding a canned infomercial down someone's throat is the way to witness to them. Such testimonies are almost always contrived. They say, "I was a rotten person. Then I invited Jesus into my heart, and now I'm nearly perfect." Although the details change from person to person, the message is as predictable as the formula for a sitcom.

This kind of witnessing is shallow, disingenuous, plastic, and probably turns off more people than it helps. But the biggest problem is this: it's not witnessing; it's a sales pitch. "Buy Jesus; He's a great deal; and you don't have to put anything down." It's like pushing a multilevel company, which benefits the promoter more than the recipient.

Because these infomercials are taught as an effective "evangelistic technique," millions believe it's what witnessing is all about; but they are mistaken. Witnessing is much deeper than that. After working at recovery for nearly three months, you should sense your experience has value beyond yourself, beyond your personal benefit. Your life—everything you do and everything you say—is a witness either for or against the Lord. He is the same Lord who has been redeeming your life from the shame, despair, depression, and worthless feelings that are a part of being abused. Because of this, wouldn't it be better to simply recognize that Christ has strengthened you with power in your inner person and everything you do is a continuous reflection of Him? If you understand this, then you know you are a witness by the life you lead, not by the words you say—and certainly not by a canned infomercial.

This kind of witnessing works, producing changed lives from the inside out. If you personify the fruit of the Spirit—love, joy, peace, patience, kindness, gentleness, faithfulness, goodness, and self-control—everything you do will have a positive impact for God as well as for everyone in your life. It's walking the walk, not just talking the talk.

Walk by the Spirit, and you will not carry out the desire of the flesh.
(GALATIANS 5:16)

Pray: Lord, give me the wisdom and discernment to "walk the walk" in purity and strength. Without Your help, all of my efforts will be shallow and fruitless. Let my life be a reflection of You, not of me.

Write: At this stage in your recovery, be careful not to become self-focused. Everything must still revolve around God and His power to work through you. Don't allow yourself to think you need to "get to work" for the Lord.

Instead continue to walk in an intimate relationship with God, delighting in Him. Once again, renew your commitment to spend at least five minutes in quiet contemplation and journaling. If you do, you'll begin to understand how every aspect of your life works together for good. Your life, which was in shambles just a few months ago, will become more focused, purposeful, and fulfilling.

Reflect

Walk by the Spirit, and you will not carry out the desire of the flesh.
For the flesh sets its desire against the Spirit, and the Spirit against
the flesh; for these are in opposition to one another, so that you may
not do the things that you please. But if you are led by the Spirit, you
are not under the Law. Now the deeds of the flesh are evident, which
are: immorality, impurity, sensuality, idolatry, sorcery, enmities, strife,
jealousy, outbursts of anger, disputes, dissensions, factions, envying,
drunkenness, carousing, and things like these, of which I forewarn
you just as I have forewarned you, that those who practice such things

will not inherit the kingdom of God. But the fruit of the Spirit is love, joy, peace, patience, kindness, goodness, faithfulness, gentleness, self-control; against such things there is no law. Now those who belong to Christ Jesus have crucified the flesh with its passions and desires.

If we live by the Spirit, let us also walk by the Spirit.

—GALATIANS 5:16–25

Accepting People

I make a commitment to nurture my relationship with God, asking
Him to reveal His will to me and to give me the power to carry it out.

Read: One of the foundational beliefs of Christianity is that human nature is sinful and separates mankind from God. Without Christ's having died for our sins, we couldn't be reconciled to God. We would be hopelessly lost forever. This is a fundamental belief of Christianity.

At the same time, Christians seem to have a profound naïveté about life. They are surprised routinely when sinful people behave in self-defeating ways.

By way of contrast, the politically correct perspective, which dominates American culture, believes mankind's nature is noble and good. When people behave poorly, however, they never seem surprised. To them, it's because these unfortunate people lack education or adequate socioeconomic opportunities. They accept most people the way they are, warts and all.

As a believer, I know there is nothing good in me, for I have a fallen nature. But I also know that when the Lord came into my life, He imparted His nature to me—full of His love, mercy, kindness, and compassion. This means I can rise above my base state to become more than I could ever hope to be without Him. This is true for every Christian. If I don't make a conscious effort to be mindful of this, however, I may become harsh and judgmental rather than merciful and kind.

This area is where Christians seem to stumble routinely. They drive away desperate people—people consumed with destructive lifestyles—refusing to give them the same compassion, kindness, and acceptance they required just a few years earlier. They embrace pride rather than humility, judgment rather than mercy, harshness rather than kindness, and rejection rather than acceptance. They cease to be like Christ, who gravitated to those who were sinful rather than to those who were self-righteous. If we are ever to be all we are capable of being, we must focus our minds on Christ and reach out to people who are badly flawed.

Halfhearted efforts to help those you consider to be beneath you will not work. In fact, it's counterproductive and comes off as holier-than-thou. Needy people see right through this attitude, rejecting this kind of "help" contemptuously. It's why they say the church is full of hypocrites, which is true. If we are ever to be who Christ intended us to be, this has to change, starting with those of us in recovery.

> *Beloved, let us love one another, for love is from God; and everyone who loves is born of God and knows God.* (1 JOHN 4:7)

Pray: Lord, show me how to love other people. Let me look at them through Your eyes, which are merciful, instead of through my eyes, which often lack compassion. Lord, renew my mind in this critical area so that I can see people as You see them.

Write: Consider what God might have you do to show love for others in your community, church, or family. Think of a specific act of kindness where you can show selfless love for someone in need. Now make plans to do it.

Reflect

> *Be hospitable to one another without complaint. As each one has received a special gift, employ it in serving one another as good stewards of the manifold grace of God. Whoever speaks, is to do so as one who is speaking the utterances of God; whoever serves is to do so as one who is serving by the strength which God supplies; so that in all things God may be glorified through Jesus Christ, to whom belongs the glory and dominion forever and ever. Amen.*
>
> —1 PETER 4:9–11

Wisdom Takes Time

I make a commitment to nurture my relationship with God, asking Him to reveal His will to me and to give me the power to carry it out.

Read: True wisdom—wisdom that comes from God—has a high price tag. If it didn't, there would be more of it. The process of gaining this precious commodity is arduous and, for the most part, intense and time-consuming.

Because we are a nation of individuals who demand instant gratification, there are fewer wise people in America than there should be. As the line from the song says, "We're older but no wiser." There is no way for fruit to mature before its season, and there is also no way to attain wisdom prematurely. It requires time, and few pursue it.

In America, you have to grow old, but you don't have to grow up. Multiplied millions never do. They're just old, having gained little wisdom in the process. Wisdom comes from weathering difficult experiences that force a person to trust the Lord completely.

Whining and blaming others may work when you're a five-year-old child, but many never seem to mature past this stage. God has no problem allowing His children to go through a world of pain, hardship, and despair to get them to where they can acquire proven character. In fact, it's standard operating procedure for Him. He does it all the time, and it can be difficult to endure.

In the short run, it may seem cruel and unfeeling. But when seen from God's perspective, which is eternal, it's absolutely necessary. It builds character—or at least it should. If He required enduring hardship from His Son, why would He require anything less from you or me?

The answer is: He wouldn't.

Therefore, when adversity comes—and it will—know that God is using every aspect of it for your benefit, your refinement, and your good. Without it, you'll never become the person you're capable of being.

> *You intended to harm me, but God intended it all for good. He brought me to this position so I could save the lives of many people.* (GENESIS 50:20 NLT)

Pray: Lord, forgive me for being a complainer most of the time. Help me learn from my experiences. Give me Your wisdom and the ability to know Your ways are always wise.

Write: If you're in the midst of difficulty, stop whining about your plight, and allow God to refine you. When it's over, you'll be stronger than you ever dreamed possible. You will be rich in Christlike qualities such as love, joy, and kindness. Above all, you'll be wise. Think of a difficult learning situation in your life, and write down a positive character quality you've developed from it.

Reflect

> *Just as it is written, "For your sake we are being put to death all day long; we were considered as sheep to be slaughtered." But in all these things we overwhelmingly conquer through Him who loved us.*
> —ROMANS 8:36–37

> *Do not complain, brethren, against one another, so that you yourselves may not be judged; behold, the Judge is standing right at the door. As an example, brethren, of suffering and patience, take the prophets who spoke in the name of the Lord. We count those blessed who endured. You have heard of the endurance of Job and have seen the outcome of the Lord's dealings, that the Lord is full of compassion and is merciful.*
> —JAMES 5:9–11

Your Life Is a Witness

I make a commitment to nurture my relationship with God, asking Him to reveal His will to me and to give me the power to carry it out.

Read: You're a witness for God in everything you do—either positively or negatively—regardless of whether you like it or not. That's just the way it is. Your life either attracts people to God or pushes them away.

For many Christians, this is intimidating. Instead they choose to become Christian automatons, who stop living life as it's meant to be lived—joyfully and spontaneously. They cease being free and instead become legalistic, punctiliously finding fault with those who don't live life as they do—straight-laced, sober, and sad. They are neither a joy to themselves nor to the Lord, which makes them difficult to be around. You know the type of person I'm describing. The church is filled with them. Their mean-spiritedness, which they wear self-righteously as a badge of virtue, repulses everyone they touch.

On the opposite spectrum are those who say, "I'm saved, so I can do anything I want." And they do. Embracing a licentious lifestyle, these Christians act like those who have no relationship with the Lord. Casting aside restraint because they're "covered," they do whatever seems right in their own eyes—regardless of the consequences to themselves or others. The church has its fair share of this type as well.

Both groups "witness for the Lord" by their lifestyles every day; they just don't realize it. The Scriptures categorize these people as "carnal" Christians. Everything about them is worldly, and the fruit of their lives doesn't attract people to God. It repulses them as it should.

The fruit of legalism is pride, faultfinding, backbiting, malice, arrogance, and by far the worst, an acerbic tongue. The fruit of licentiousness is sensuality, sexual immorality, alcoholism, consumptive materialism, gluttony, and greed.

216

If you fall into either of these groups, there is hope. God wants more for your life than wasting it as a self-righteous bigot or a lascivious philanderer. The way to change is easy, but doing the consistent work necessary to be the man or woman Christ intended you to be isn't. It takes consistent effort.

Jesus said to him, "I am the way, and the truth, and the life; no one comes to the Father but through Me." (JOHN 14:6)

Pray: Father, please open my eyes to all the ways I've been living. Show me where I have been self-defeating in my thoughts and actions. Cleanse me and lead me in the fruitful, honorable way.

Write: Look to God to show you what He wants in your life rather than making your assumptions about His will. We serve a radical God. Often what I think He wants is different from what He truly wants. Nearness to God is the key. What do you think is your next step in recovery? Write it out and ask God if it really is His will or just a noble projection of your mind.

Reflect

For this reason also, since the day we heard of it, we have not ceased to pray for you and to ask that you may be filled with the knowledge of His will in all spiritual wisdom and understanding, so that you will walk in a manner worthy of the Lord, to please Him in all respects, bearing fruit in every good work and increasing in the knowledge of God; strengthened with all power, according to His glorious might, for the attaining of all steadfastness and patience; joyously giving thanks to the Father, who has qualified us to share in the inheritance of the saints in Light.

—COLOSSIANS 1:9–12

You'll Know Them by Their Love

I make a commitment to nurture my relationship with God, asking Him to reveal His will to me and to give me the power to carry it out.

Read: I remember having lunch with a man many years ago. When it came time to pay the bill, he left a tract about Christ rather than a tip. He said, "I'm giving the waitress 'a chance' at eternal life, which is far more valuable than leaving her a couple of bucks." He really did this, and the worst part was that he believed the nonsense he was spouting. After he left, I doubled my tip; so the young lady wouldn't blame God for this man's penny-pinching faux pas.

As a result of this event, I asked God to show me every time I was unkind, knowing He might be blamed for my insensitivity. It's a prayer that has been answered in spades many times, and I've had to make amends to people numerous times. By doing this, however, I've learned that people are attracted to Christ by kindness, mercy, love, and acceptance—not tracts or hollow, judgmental platitudes.

Isn't His love, acceptance, and mercy what drew you to Him?

When someone told me God loved me in spite of my difficulty, my heart melted—and so did my resistance.

In me, the fruit was real when I first believed in Christ decades ago, but it still required years for me to mature. The Lord has been very patient with me—unlike some self-righteous Christians. He is patient with all of His children. It's because He wants each of us to be everything we're capable of being; and for some of us, it takes a long time.

In Psalm 1, the tree planted by running water yielded its fruit "in its season" and not before. That's why we have to be merciful with our Christian friends, especially with those who have been abused. Their fruit may not yet be ready, and there's no way to make it ready before its season. Green fruit is sour and not sweet, and it's usually hard to digest. When it's mature, however, nothing is tastier or more satisfying.

> *How blessed is the man who does not walk in the counsel of the wicked,*
>   *Nor stand in the path of sinners,*
>   *Nor sit in the seat of scoffers!*
> *But his delight is in the law of the LORD,*
>   *And in His law he meditates day and night.*
> *He will be like a tree firmly planted by streams of water,*
>   *Which yields its fruit in its season*
>   *And its leaf does not wither;*
>   *And in whatever he does, he prospers.* (PSALM 1:1–3)

Pray: Lord, help me be merciful with myself and with others. Remind me that You have begun a good work in me, a work You intend to complete. Help me also recognize that You are working in the lives of others. Help me be like You—loving, patient, and kind.

Write: Be open to what God wants to do through you. It is not about "doing" what you think God wants, but "being" open to His direction. If anything has already come to your mind, write it down. If not, ask God to use you, and see what happens.

Reflect

> *God, being rich in mercy, because of His great love with which He loved us even when we were dead in our transgressions, made us alive together with Christ (by grace you have been saved), and raised us up with Him, and seated us with Him in the heavenly places in Christ Jesus, so that in the ages to come He might show the surpassing riches of His grace in kindness toward us in Christ Jesus.*
>
> *—EPHESIANS 2:4–7*

> *When the kindness of God our Savior and His love for mankind appeared, He saved us, not on the basis of deeds which we have done in righteousness, but according to His mercy, by the washing of*

regeneration and renewing by the Holy Spirit, whom He poured out upon us richly through Jesus Christ our Savior, so that being justified by His grace we would be made heirs according to the hope of eternal life.

—TITUS 3:4–7

A NEW LIFE

Introduction

Having completed the 11 steps, you are now prepared to move forward in life confidently, knowing God has freed you from a spirit of fear and from feelings of shame and low self-esteem. He has replaced these debilitating emotions with a spirit of love, power, and sound judgment. You are free, and nothing need ever hinder you again. That's what recovery is all about, living life as it's meant to be lived—free from fear and shame.

You now are empowered to be everything you are capable of being. Having a sober spirit, you can comprehend the deep love God has for you. Those who sought your destruction have failed miserably, as your resurgence to emotional health testifies. Your heavenly Father made certain of it. He reached down and lifted you out of your prison, out of your despair and disillusionment. Now that your eyes have been opened, it will be much more difficult for an abusive person to ever deceive you again.

By now, you probably understand the true depth of God's love for you—a love that was unwilling to allow you to wallow in self-defeating behavior any longer.

As the final week of *Recovering from Religious Abuse* begins, we will look at your life beyond intense recovery to a life that smiles at the future rather than grimaces because of the past. Once you've finished this week, you will be prepared to help others in their recovery. Many are plagued with the crushing sense of hopelessness brought on by abuse; and you are well able to be there for someone who needs a guide, a knowledgeable confidant.

That person can be you. In fact, it should be you. You can be a blessing to someone else; and when you are, life will have more meaning than you can imagine.

Be Exceptional in Ordinary Things

Read: There is something in each of us that wants to be heroic, noble, and above all, admired. It's a part of human nature—a characteristic common to all. Having completed the 11 steps, perhaps the thought has occurred to you that your time has finally come—your time to shine in the sun—to be acclaimed and broadly admired.

If that's a thought you've entertained, you're correct to have done so. As you make strides in your recovery, God is strengthening you with power in the inner person. He is molding you to be the man or woman He always intended you to be. If you continue, you undoubtedly will achieve more than you ever dreamed possible and become a person rich in estimable character qualities. Your influence will expand, but it's unlikely you will ever see the full scope of your impact. You're not intended to; it's not God's way. It would puff you up, and that's not what He desires.

The trick is for you to see life as God sees it—not for Him to see it as you think it should be. In our natural state, we want to be exceptional, noticed by those around us as several cuts above the ordinary. It's our calling—we're certain of it—and we want everybody to notice. God's criteria for success is different. He wants us to cultivate faithfulness and allow Him to be responsible for everything else.

He wants us to keep our eyes on Him, not on our accomplishments. It's why He orchestrates our lives so carefully, keeping us from measuring the good we've done. It goes largely unnoticed—except in His eyes. He sees what you've done, and He knows the state of your heart when you did it. If you do something for public acclaim, you've obtained all the value you will ever receive from it. If, on the other hand, you are exceptional in the way you do ordinary things, you become a colaborer with God Himself, and the fruit of your actions will be incalculable, creating blessings that will transcend generations. That's what has eternal value.

I am well content with weaknesses, with insults, with distresses, with persecutions, with difficulties, for Christ's sake; for when I am weak, then I am strong. (2 CORINTHIANS 12:10)

Pray: Father, help me to be faithful with what You give me to do. Help me understand the experiences You have orchestrated in my life—even the abuse. Show me how You want to use my experiences to benefit others. Use what You've put in me through recovery to have eternal value.

Write: Take five minutes to be still before God. Ask Him to give you the ability to hear His voice as He leads you. Be open to follow the direction He shows you. If something seems clear, take a minute to write it down and place it where you can see it regularly—perhaps on the refrigerator or closet door. If it's from God, it will become clearer as each day passes.

Reflect

He rejoiced greatly in the Holy Spirit, and said, "I praise You, O Father, Lord of heaven and earth, that You have hidden these things from the wise and intelligent and have revealed them to infants. Yes, Father, for this way was well-pleasing in Your sight."

—LUKE 10:21

The secret of the LORD is for those who fear Him,
And He will make them know His covenant.
My eyes are continually toward the LORD,
For He will pluck my feet out of the net.
Turn to me and be gracious to me,
For I am lonely and afflicted.

PSALM 25:14–16

God Is in Control

Read: Jesus lived a simple life. Nothing about it was grandiose, and He made no attempt to exalt Himself. He was perfectly content to leave the outcome of His work in His Father's hands, which is exactly what we are learning to do in recovery—one day at a time. Christ wasn't wealthy, and He eschewed materialism. To Jesus, doing His Father's will was the only mark of success. Two millennia later, nothing has changed. Success is doing God's will—nothing more, nothing less.

In our natural state, we want to control the outcome of our lives, and we foolishly believe we can. But life doesn't work that way—never has, never will. The outcome is in God's hands, not ours. I can't control the future and neither can you. It's not our job. We don't even get a vote.

Through substantial reflection and introspection, you have learned to take responsibility for your actions and to forgive the behavior of others, including those who abused you. Each step in this process was necessary to prepare you for the future. By working the 11 steps, you have purged most of the toxic emotions that enslaved you to self-defeating behavior. By facing your fear, shame, and anger, you have freed yourself to walk into the future without the need to medicate the pain from your past with alcohol, drugs, pornography, promiscuity, overeating, or any other destructive thing.

You are free to become the person God always intended for you to be. Instead of dreading the future, you can get up each morning and smile at what life has in store for you—regardless of how difficult your situation may be. Through daily prayer and reflection, you can keep your recovery fresh and know God will always be with you. He has your back—no matter what.

Be strong and courageous, do not be afraid or tremble at them, for the LORD your God is the one who goes with you. He will not fail you or forsake you. (DEUTERONOMY 31:6)

Pray: Father, the outcome of my life and my recovery is in Your hands. Please give me the grace to let go and allow You to be fully in control. When I'm tempted to take it back, remind me of how badly I've always handled being in charge.

Write: As you reflect over the past twelve weeks of recovery, what has God been teaching you about yourself? What has He been teaching you about your recovery? Most important, what have you learned about your heavenly Father? Take some time to journal on these reflections.

Reflect

"I know the plans that I have for you," declares the LORD, "plans for welfare and not for calamity to give you a future and a hope. Then you will call upon Me and come and pray to Me, and I will listen to you."

—JEREMIAH 29:11–12

Commit your works to the LORD
And your plans will be established.

—PROVERBS 16:3

Value Beyond Yourself

Read: During the past eighty-seven days, the focus of each day's reading has been on you and your recovery. Each devotional has been introspective, taking a penetrating look at the painful events surrounding your abusive experience. The goal has been to help you move beyond the place where your emotional growth stagnated—the place where you were used, abused, and discarded. Without taking an incisive look at everything surrounding the events of your abuse, no healing would have been possible. You would have remained stuck—unable to move forward, unable to achieve fulfillment.

Now that this has been accomplished, the focal point needs to change. It needs to shift outward rather than inward—toward others rather than toward you. Being introspective has had its place, but to continue looking inward shouldn't be your exclusive focus.

Your recovery has value beyond yourself—at least as far as God is concerned. He has healed you for His reasons as well as for your own. Having achieved substantial healing from your abuse, God wants your experience to benefit others—those who remain stuck in such toxic emotions as anger, bitterness, shame, and low self-esteem.

Having just been through the recovery process—having looked at yourself in depth—there's nobody better than you to help someone who is suffering from the same debilitating emotions. That's why your experience is so valuable. You can help someone else, just like you've been helped.

When you do, the joy you experience will be beyond measure. Everything, including the air you breathe, will seem sweeter. Perhaps for the first time in your life, you will know beyond a doubt you have done the right thing at the right time for the right reason. You will have helped another find joy and a life worth living. As far as accomplishments are concerned, it doesn't get any better than that.

*Jesus replied, "You must love the L*ORD *your God with all your heart, all your soul, and all your mind." This is the first and greatest commandment. A second is equally important: "Love your neighbor as yourself."* (MATTHEW 22:37–39 NLT).

Pray: God, help me begin to look outward rather than exclusively inward. Give me a heart to help other people. Guide me as I reach out to others.

Write: Be open to how God wants to use you in the lives of others—those who remain trapped by toxic emotions and low self-esteem. Make a list of people you know whom you may be able to reach out to. You don't have to force this to happen. All you have to do is be open and ready for God to use you when the time is right.

Reflect

He saved us, not on the basis of deeds which we have done in righteousness, but according to His mercy, by the washing of regeneration and renewing by the Holy Spirit, whom He poured out upon us richly through Jesus Christ our Savior, so that being justified by His grace we would be made heirs according to the hope of eternal life. This is a trustworthy statement; and concerning these things I want you to speak confidently, so that those who have believed God will be careful to engage in good deeds. These things are good and profitable for men. But avoid foolish controversies and genealogies and strife and disputes about the Law, for they are unprofitable and worthless.

—TITUS 3:5–9

Keeping Your Eyes Open

Read: Although you may not recognize it, you're a much more insightful person than you were three months ago. Because of the heartache you've endured and your willingness to take a penetrating look at the painful events surrounding your abuse, you have learned recovery skills that will help you live life successfully. Unlike most, you can now look at yourself more realistically than ever before.

Because abuse is so personal and such an affront, you may believe your experience is unique, that nobody has ever suffered as unjustly as you. But, when you think about it, you recognize this isn't true, don't you?

Sadly, religious abuse is quite common. Millions have suffered from it—exactly like you. Most haven't even considered the need for a recovery program, which means you now possess something they don't. You know a way out; you know about the 11 steps. Most don't have a clue about how to recover from their abuse. They're still grinding out their days, suffering from shame, low self-esteem, and disillusionment.

This is what makes you special. You are in a unique position to help others, just as you've been helped. All you have to do is keep your eyes open and your senses aware. God will bring as many people into your life as you have the capacity to help—perhaps more. The problem is enormous, and those who are capable of helping are so few.

Be vigilant. Be open. Be available. Regardless of what you're involved in, helping others discover the freedom you now enjoy is a part of your new life and will remain so from now on.

Even when we are weighed down with troubles, it is for your comfort and salvation! For when we ourselves are comforted, we will certainly comfort you. Then you can patiently endure the same things we suffer. We are confident that as you share in our sufferings, you will also share in the comfort God gives us. (2 CORINTHIANS 1:6–7 NLT)

Pray: Father, open my eyes to recognize the needs of those around me. Let me look at others as You see them. Please show me those You want me to help with their recovery.

Write: There are people out there who have been through experiences similar to yours but who remain trapped by their past, by their anger and their shame. Ask God to bring people like this into your path. Can you think of those who fit these criteria? Begin praying for them, and ask God if you should possibly even contact them. Write down specific ways you can be open to what is in store for you, and be alert to those who cross your path.

Reflect

Teach those who are rich in this world not to be proud and not to trust in their money, which is so unreliable. Their trust should be in God, who richly gives us all we need for our enjoyment. Tell them to use their money to do good. They should be rich in good works and generous to those in need, always being ready to share with others. By doing this they will be storing up their treasure as a good foundation for the future so that they may experience true life.
                                                    —1 TIMOTHY 6:17–19 NLT

When You Regress

Read: For the past three months, you've made substantial growth as you've begun to heal from the pain of your religious abuse. Because you've grown so much and so quickly, you may think continuous growth will be the norm. I wish this were true, but it isn't.

You'll have periods of regression, periods where you'll doubt you've made any growth at all—periods where none of your recovery will seem real. When this happens, stop what you're doing and take a spot inventory. Be introspective once again. Ask yourself the same hard questions you asked early in your recovery about your feelings and your behavior:

- What is different today than yesterday?
- What is causing your disquietude?
- What have you been doing that you shouldn't have been doing?
- What haven't you been doing that you should have been doing?
- What is your emotional state?
- What is happening with others that's impacting your recovery?

Whatever it is, address it and correct it at once. Think of it like the instructions you receive before every commercial flight. The attendant warns you to put the oxygen mask on yourself first and then on your children. The reason is obvious. If you don't take care of yourself, you can't possibly take care of others.

It's the same with recovery. You must take care of yourself, or you'll never be able to take care of others. You have to maintain your recovery above all else.

When you discover the problem, do whatever is necessary to correct the situation and get back on track. Remember, your value to yourself and to others is only as good as the quality of your spiritual state, which is dependent upon the state of your recovery. Take care of it, and it will take care of everything else.

If we confess our sins, He is faithful and righteous to forgive us our sins and to cleanse us from all unrighteousness. (1 JOHN 1:9)

Pray: Father, show me how to deal with the times I'm not making progress in my recovery. Help me be gentle with myself when this happens rather than critical. Remind me that I'm pursuing progress, not perfection.

Write: How are you doing today? Take time to do a spot inventory as described above. Use the techniques you learned in step 7 and write about what's going on. You can also review what you wrote in step 7. If you find yourself off track, correct the situation by relying on the Lord to take control of that problem. Remember, the key is to pursue progress rather than perfection.

Reflect

We will speak the truth in love, growing in every way more and more like Christ, who is the head of his body, the church. He makes the whole body fit together perfectly. As each part does its own special work, it helps the other parts grow, so that the whole body is healthy and growing and full of love.

—EPHESIANS 4:15–16 NLT

Humble yourselves under the mighty hand of God, that He may exalt you at the proper time, casting all your anxiety on Him, because He cares for you.

1 PETER 5:6–7

What's Next?

Read: As you complete your 91-day commitment, you probably have mixed feelings. You're relieved it's over, but you're already apprehensive about the future—about how to keep your recovery moving in the right direction.

The good news is that the Lord is always available to you, and He's definitely on your side. You and your recovery are near and dear to Him—that's for certain. You can become everything in life God ever intended you to be, and you need never be debilitated by feelings of shame and worthlessness again. Even if you have a bad day or two, you can discover the problem and work the appropriate step to correct the situation. It's as easy as that.

Nothing need hinder your progress—nothing. You're a beloved child of God, and you have instant access to your heavenly Father, regardless of the situation. Nobody can take that away from you; nobody has that authority or that right.

You can look at your recovery with profound satisfaction, and the future can be filled with good things. Your life may have blessings beyond measure. God's plan for your life has not changed nor has His love for you.

Remember, He wants good things for you, not bad things. You're richer in character than you've ever been, and each day you can become a better person. All you have to do is want it and be willing to work for it.

"I know the plans that I have for you," declares the LORD, "plans for welfare and not for calamity to give you a future and a hope."
(JEREMIAH 29:11)

Pray: God, enable me to keep my recovery moving in the right direction. Above all else, help me to keep my eyes on You. Thank You for being there for me, for loving me exactly the way I am.

Write: What does "working your recovery" look like from this point forward? Come up with a clear action plan to stay in touch with the 11 steps. Go one step further and write it down. The steps will aid you stay on the positive path to healing and recovery. Now go and work your plan. It will work if you work it.

Reflect

Look at the ravens. They don't plant or harvest or store food in barns, for God feeds them. And you are far more valuable to him than any birds! Can all your worries add a single moment to your life? And if worry can't accomplish a little thing like that, what's the use of worrying over bigger things?

Look at the lilies and how they grow. They don't work or make their clothing, yet Solomon in all his glory was not dressed as beautifully as they are. And if God cares so wonderfully for flowers that are here today and thrown into the fire tomorrow, he will certainly care for you. Why do you have so little faith?

—LUKE 12:24–28 NLT

Be anxious for nothing, but in everything by prayer and supplication with thanksgiving let your requests be made known to God. And the peace of God, which surpasses all comprehension, will guard your hearts and your minds in Christ Jesus.

—PHILIPPIANS 4:6–7

MOVING FORWARD

You've gained strength and insight as you've worked the 11 steps. Now it's your turn to help others. You've done the work, but if you want to keep it, you must pass it on. If you give it away, you'll be enriched. If you hoard it, the growth you've achieved will atrophy.

Others need what you have. If you want your joy and freedom to be complete, help someone else. There's nothing like it. There's no reward greater than helping another. Try it; you'll see for yourself. It's the final step necessary to be:

The person you were created to be,

the person you've always wanted to be,

the person God intended you to be.

ACKNOWLEDGMENTS

I want to thank Louisa McCullough Tremann, who has assisted me from Day One. Without her help and her keen eye, I would still be writing the manuscript. I would also like to thank my friend of twenty-five years, Jonathan Merkh, who believed in me and chose to give me a chance. Gary McCauley, who has been my friend since the early '80s, encouraged me each step of the way, providing consistent support. A special thanks also goes to Robert McGee, who has been my active champion. A special thanks to Heather and to my family—especially Katie, the Kerlins, and the Mixons—for their support

My editorial team at Howard Books has been great, including Philis Boultinghouse, Jessica Wong, and Becky Nesbitt. I would also like to say thanks to Cindy Lambert, Greg Petree, and Denny Boultinghouse—each of whom has assisted me along the way. Finally, I would like to thank my literary agent, who is also my friend, Wes Yoder.